P9-CQE-266

Searching
the Prophets
for Values

BALFOUR BRICKNER and ALBERT VORSPAN

Searching
the Prophets
for Values

Union of American Hebrew Congregations
New York

Copyright © 1981
by Balfour Brickner and Albert Vorspan

Library of Congress Cataloging in Publication Data
Brickner, Balfour,
   Searching the prophets for values.
   SUMMARY: Approaches the study of the Prophets
by presenting the values they espoused.
   1. Bible. O.T. Prophets–Text-books.
   2. Bible. O.T. Former Prophets–Text-books.
   3. Prophets–Study and teaching (Secondary)
[1. Prophets. 2. Ethics, Jewish] I. Vorspan, Albert,
joint author. II. Title.
BS1286.B74   222   81-419
ISBN 0-8074-0047-5   AACR1

Manufactured in the United States of America

2 3 4 5 6 7 8 9 0

SINCE IT WOULD be the most arrogant chutzpah for us to dedicate this book to the prophets of Israel–they hardly need our tribute–we dedicate this book, in full humility, to each other.

Frankly, we do need it and we think we deserve it. After over two decades of closest personal friendship and professional association, and after a decade of work since the idea for this book was first discussed, we know we need and deserve each other.

UNLIKE OTHER TEXTS teaching the "prophets," this one, fashioned for teenagers, approaches them through the values they championed rather than through a study of the history of their times. We have tried to relate these values to the ethical problems young people meet in their everyday lives.

This text cannot be explored fully without the Bible which is its indispensable companion.

We would like to thank the people who helped and supported us in the preparation of this book. We are especially grateful to Rabbi Daniel B. Syme, director of education, for his encouragement and his unflagging enthusiasm. He extended his support every step of the way, sometimes when our spirits lagged a little. For extremely helpful criticism and comment on the various stages of the manuscript, we express our gratitude to Rabbis Bernard Zlotowitz, Henry Cohen, Roland B. Gittelsohn, and Steven Reuben, and to Mrs. Edith Samuel ז״ל . For their patience in typing, we thank Ruth Harrison and Vivian Mendeles; for their copy editing, Josette Knight and Esther Fried Africk; and for shepherding the book through the many stages of publication, Ralph Davis and Stuart Benick.

B.B.
A.V.

Contents

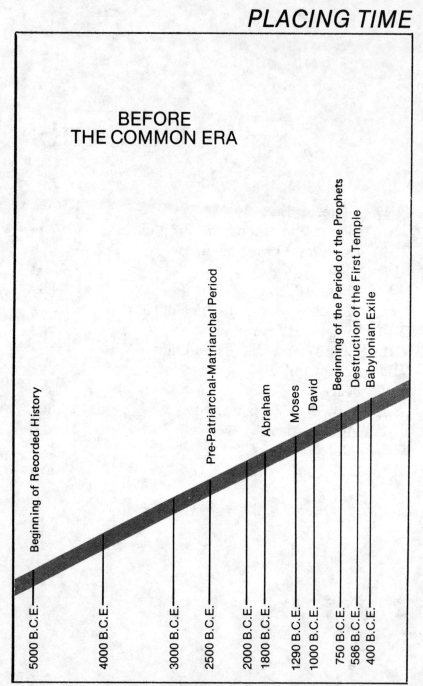

**BEFORE
THE COMMON ERA**

Beginning of Recorded History

Pre-Patriarchal-Matriarchal Period

Abraham

Moses

David

Beginning of the Period of the Prophets

Destruction of the First Temple

Babylonian Exile

5000 B.C.E.

4000 B.C.E.

3000 B.C.E.

2500 B.C.E.

2000 B.C.E.

1800 B.C.E.

1290 B.C.E.

1000 B.C.E.

750 B.C.E.

586 B.C.E.

400 B.C.E.

Note that Jewish history is recorded for approximately

IN PERSPECTIVE

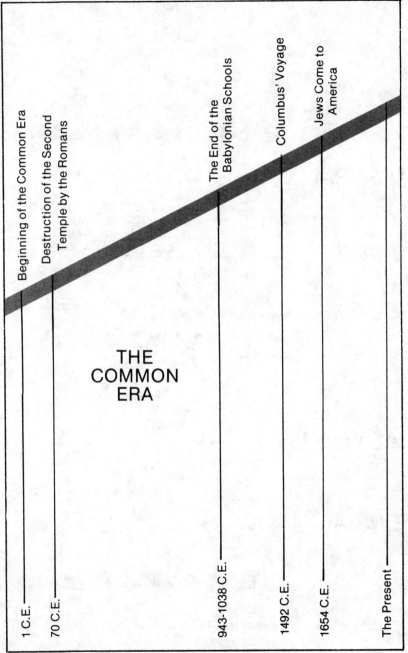

Beginning of the Common Era

Destruction of the Second Temple by the Romans

The End of the Babylonian Schools

Columbus' Voyage

Jews Come to America

THE COMMON ERA

1 C.E.

70 C.E.

943-1038 C.E.

1492 C.E.

1654 C.E.

The Present

twice as long as the history of Western civilization.

MAJOR EVENTS, PERSONALITIES,

800 B.C.E.   700 B.C.E.

ASSYRIA

Tiglath-Pilezer III 744-727

Siege of Samaria 722-721
Sargon II 722-705
Sennacherib 705-681

ISRAEL

Jeroboam II 783-749
Amos 750
Hosea 745

JUDAH

Amaziah 798-780
Syro-Israelite Alliance 734
Ahaz 731-727
Isaiah I 742-700
Micah 757-700
Hezekiah 715-687

BABYLONIA

Rise of Babylonia

PERSIA

800 B.C.E.   700 B.C.E.

NATIONS DURING TIME OF PROPHETS

Josiah 640-609
  Jeremiah 626-587
    Habakuk 612
     Jehoiakim 609-598
      Babylonian Captivity 587-586
     Ezekiel 592-570
      Haggai & Zechariah 586
     Second Isaiah 540
      Rebuilding the Temple 520-515

Nebuchadnezzar 625-562
  Edict of Cyrus 538

Rise of Persia 584 or 589
      Darius 521-486

Malachi 500-450
  Ezra's Mission 458(?)
   Nehemiah 445
    Ezra's Mission 428(?)

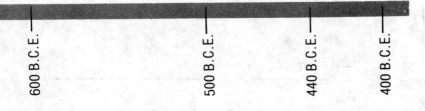

WHEN DID THE PROPHETS LIVE?

516 B.C.E.————— Malachi

586 B.C.E.————— Babylonian Exile • Jeremiah • Ezekiel •
Deuteronomy • Deutero-Isaiah • Haggai • Zechariah

612 B.C.E.————— Habakuk

722 B.C.E.————— Fall of Northern Kingdom • Joel • Obadiah •
Nahum • Zephaniah

750 B.C.E.————— Amos • Hosea • Isaiah I

1000 B.C.E.————— Davidic Age   • Nathan

1290 B.C.E.————— Moses and the Exodus

1800 B.C.E.————— Abraham

Editor's Introduction

For more than three decades, most Jewish students have studied the prophets during intermediate or junior high years. Texts treating the subject have almost invariably been organized around the personalities of these prophetic figures, giving their biographies and offering selected "great passages" from their writings.

But the true greatness of the prophets, and the source of their enduring influence on humankind, is not so much their words, but rather the values they espoused. Accordingly, a text designed to present the prophets in terms of their real significance should embody a values-centered orientation.

In *Searching the Prophets for Values,* Albert Vorspan and Balfour Brickner make a significant breakthrough in the systematic presentation of prophetic teachings. Gearing their work to a more mature high school and adult audience capable of greater conceptual understanding, they have enabled the study of Amos, Isaiah, Micah, Jeremiah to be brought to life in relation to the values which shaped their lives.

Moreover, the authors employ an organizing principle that starts with a basic Jewish value, illustrating how each prophet addressed it. Finally, Vorspan and Brickner bridge the gap between the ancient and modern world by showing how sorely our contemporary society needs to embrace those same ethical teachings, first articulated over 2,000 years ago.

We hope that you will find this book a valued addition to your personal Jewish library, whether in the classroom or in your home. It is yet another demonstration of the power and eternal significance of our Jewish heritage.

RABBI DANIEL B. SYME

Searching the Prophets for Values

Values
to Live By

D ID you ever hear of a *Golem?*

Have you ever heard of a Jewish Frankenstein?

Few stories have stirred the Jewish imagination as profoundly as the incredible tale of the Golem. It has provided the basis for several plays and operas. The German silent motion picture, *The Golem,* was one of the screen's earliest horror movies, and possibly served as the prototype for the film classic, *Frankenstein.* The legend of the Golem has probably inspired more than its share of prayers, dreams, and nightmares.

The most popular Golem story had its origin in seventeenth-century Czechoslovakia. Life for Jews in that European country was grim. Persecution of Jews ranged from daily verbal humiliation to rampaging mobs who beat up Jewish men, women, and children. A defenseless, miserable Jewish community sought some escape from the terror of a hostile and cruel people. As Jews have done through the centuries, they turned to their rabbi—in this case, the great Rabbi Judah Loew, who was known as something of a miracle worker.

And, the story is told, Rabbi Loew of Prague provided them with the defense they needed. One night, he and two of his companions went down to the Moldau (Czech Vlatava) River outside of the city and gathered up a quantity of mud from the river bank. There they fashioned a Golem, a giant figure in the shape of a man. The Golem was still only clay until Rabbi Loew inserted a small parchment under its tongue on which he had written *yod hei vov hei,* the four Hebrew letters that spell *Adonai,* the Hebrew word for God. According to the legend, at that moment the giant Golem stirred and came to life, thereafter obeying every command given it by the saintly rabbi. Each night Rabbi Loew instructed the Golem to walk the streets of the ghetto of Prague and to protect its Jewish residents from whatever danger might befall.

Like a good monster, the Golem reported and made its rounds, frightening away a would-be attacker here, dispersing a mob of hoodlums there, intercepting an assassin or a thief in another quarter. The word spread quickly through the entire community that a frightful monster roamed the streets of the Jewish quarter, protecting the Jews.

Life for the Jews of that community improved quickly. Calm and a sense of safety again prevailed. Each morning at dawn, upon the rabbi's command, the Golem would return to the rabbi's house. The clay giant would lie inert all day in the corner on a pile of worn-out and discarded books. What eventually happened to the Golem, how it ran amok, and why the rabbi destroyed it are all part of the long and fanciful legend which can be read elsewhere. But the story does raise a question which we would like to consider with you.

If you had the magical power to create a humanlike character, as the rabbi of Prague is reputed to have done, what qualities would you put into such a creature? (By the way, it may not be as outlandish a question as it seems. Scientists working on the frontiers of biological and physical research have already discovered ways through which to effect genetic changes in living organisms. Humankind is now on the brink of creating new forms of life—our own Golems?—and the possibility is so awesome that high-ranking biologists have called for a halt to certain kinds of research in order to evaluate the implications of this new, and in some ways frightening, knowledge.)

Would you give your character extraordinary physical strength? Would you make such a person exceptionally beautiful or handsome? Intellectually brilliant? Witty? Would such a person be a truth teller? A peace lover? Always just?

Most people would argue that, while the first two qualities might be desirable, the last three are critically important. In other words, they would create a person with positive moral values, an individual with a *moral identity*.

Everyone has a moral identity of one kind or another. For some it is negative: "You can't trust him," "She's a habitual liar," "She's a crook," "I wouldn't trust him as far as I can throw him." Some other people we view positively: "You can count on her," "She's as honest as the day is long," "She's a really loving person," "He cares," "He wouldn't hurt a fly." Your classmates and friends make these kinds of value judgments about you all the time, and you do the same about them. All human beings judge and are judged in terms of the values they hold and express in their lives. Every one of us has an individual moral identity. It is the most important thing that can be said about us, even more important than what we look like, whether or not we are physically strong or weak, good or poor athletes, good or poor students, brave or cowardly.

There is a Midrash (an early rabbinic comment on a biblical text) that tells us that all people really have three names. One our parents give us. One our friends call us. And one we earn ourselves. It's that last name, our moral reputation or identity, that this book is all about.

How does one form a moral identity?

Surely, no one is born with one. We are all born morally neutral, neither good nor bad, just nor unjust, kind nor cruel, sensitive nor insensitive, weak nor courageous. These qualities develop as we grow. Some people never develop a positive moral identity. Some end up being "no good" all their lives. Because of such people we have to have police forces, locks on our doors, even armies to protect a nation from

other nations which would destroy a neighboring society.
Countries, too, develop moral identities. What is America's?
Does it change? Has Germany's? Japan's? Israel's?

On the other hand, some people become tremendous
forces for good in their communities, their world. What
makes some people trustworthy, decent, law-abiding, sensitive to the needs of others, while other people become de-
ceptive, cruel, filled with hate, spoiling for a fight, and totally
destructive? No one really knows the complete answer to
that most difficult question, but we do know some of the
elements which go into forming a person's moral identity.

ENVIRONMENT

The environment in which a person lives and grows has a lot
to do with how a person develops morally. It is more difficult
for a child to develop a positive moral identity when he or
she is forced to grow up in a slum and to fight and scratch
for survival than it is if a child grows up in a situation where
the basic physical and social needs of life are provided. We
also know that a young person who grows up without love
and demonstrated affection is more likely to become selfish
and insensitive to others than one raised in a social situation
where love is present and affection freely given. We know
that a decent education has a lot to do with the development
of the values by which people live as they become adults.
There is more crime, more brutality, greater disregard for
human life among those who are deprived than there is
among those who grow up in favorable conditions. But poverty is not the only factor that determines a person's moral
identity.

Increasingly, we discover that young people from well-
to-do homes sometimes do terrifying and horrible things.
Some time ago three young adults, all from very wealthy
homes, kidnapped a busful of children in a small community
in California and buried the bus, with the children and

driver, in an abandoned stone quarry owned by one of the men's fathers. They did this partly as a lark, partly to see if they could get money from the parents of the children. Why? What went haywire in the minds of these three young men that caused them even to consider such a terrible deed? Whatever it was, it did not come out of the blue. It came from particular moral identities shaped by particular values—or the absence of them.

What is a *value?* How is it formed? How are values applied? How do we make right or wrong, good or bad decisions?

Obviously, reading about and understanding values won't necessarily cause us to live our lives by them. That requires a conscious will to be moral and the discipline to act accordingly. The two key words are *will* and *action.* People judge you, even as you judge people, by what you do or do not do, not merely by what you say. Based on that, your friends and ultimately the larger society will make a judgment about you, will stamp you with a moral identity. That identity will shape your life in ways you cannot possibly fathom. It will determine whether you get one kind of job or another, whether or not you are chosen for a position of responsibility, the kind of mate you have, the kind of children you raise; in short, whether or not you become what is generally called successful or happy. Are values important? Clearly, they are.

LEARNING AND ACQUIRING VALUES

How do we acquire values? There are several ways. The first is, of course, through what we are taught. Since no one is born with a sense of values, just as no one is born with a moral identity, we have to have it given to us—*taught* to us.

George Santayana once wrote: "Those who cannot remember the past are condemned to repeat it." In other words, the past, which we sometimes call experience or history, is a great teacher. People have been living on this planet for thousands of years. We have pretty complete records of what they did and didn't do, the mistakes they made, as well as the wise choices they made. We know what has caused pain, brought grief, destroyed trust between individuals and nations over the centuries. And since most of us try to avoid pain, grief, and the loss of trust, it is only sensible to look at the past and try to learn from the mistakes previous generations made so we don't make them again. If we don't learn, we just end up making our own lives that much less pleasurable. History is certainly one way to learn what is and what is not ethically or morally valuable.

For many people, the real way of learning values is through the test of personal experience. We see the effects of what we do or don't do. Trial and error is a wasteful way to learn, but every generation, it seems, thinks it has to reinvent the wheel.

Other people, by the force of their examples, may inspire values in us. We call people whose lives we wish to emulate "role models." Once we called them heroes. When flying was an audacious challenge, Charles Lindbergh (the first person to fly solo across the Atlantic Ocean) and Amelia Earhardt were heroes to millions of people who knew only that they also wanted to conquer the sky. And how many young women drew their inspiration for political activism from the courageous example of Golda Meir? Clarence Darrow, the famous trial lawyer, was the role model for thousands of aspiring young attorneys. Every career, every profession, every vocation has had its heroes, heroines, or role models upon whom those who have tried to follow have patterned themselves.

Can you imagine anyone who lived in the days of King David, or the prophets Amos or Jeremiah, using them as their role models? Do you try to pattern yourself after the life-style of another person or persons? One of the complaints commonly heard in adult circles nowadays is that there are so few positive role models after whom young people can pattern themselves. Do you think that is true? Who are your role models, the heroes or heroines whom you would want to be like? What are their values? Or are they all only momentary celebrities whose fame vanishes with the wind of the newest fad? Is there a difference between a true role model and a celebrity? If so, what are the characteristics that distinguish the two?

For some, there is another way of acquiring values: by believing they know what their God wants. At one time, most people believed that God would punish or reward them for their actions. If you told the truth, acted honestly, behaved with fairness toward others, did not cheat, murder, or steal, God would reward you with eternal life in some heaven someplace. And if you acted in the opposite fashion, God would punish you with an afterlife in some terrible place called hell. While there are still lots of people who continue to believe in that simple approach, most people have matured beyond such an innocent understanding. Certainly Reform Judaism does not teach such a doctrine.

Most of us no longer think of heaven or hell as places to which people go after they die. Also, because we see values in conflict with each other, we are no longer so certain about what God wants. Additionally, we see too many people who quite successfully seem to get away with violating what are called God's laws. Finally, there are lots of people who have given up their belief in God altogether, precisely because God has been so much identified with reward and punishment. Many people now tend to think of God in totally different ways: as a Force or Power that motivates people to do and be better. Thought of in these terms, God becomes the greatest of all "oughts"—the highest, finest, most noble standard to which we can aspire, the yardstick against which we measure all our thoughts and actions. Certainly, to try to give to God that ultimate place in our thinking is to make God a source of values in the finest, and perhaps the most demanding, way.

The Jewish tradition tries to do just that. The people are

commanded to be holy. Why? "For I, the Lord your God, am holy" (Lev. 19:2). In other words, be like (imitate) God. The tradition then carefully defines what it means by holiness. Notice that this word is not left fuzzy. On the contrary, the Hebrew Bible is very specific about what it considers holiness to be. Notice, too, that holiness is not defined solely in terms of prayer or worship. Holiness in the Jewish tradition is a demand to do. It is an action, often a social action, including such specifics as:

Respecting parents

Keeping the Shabbat

Leaving the gleanings of the harvest and the ungathered grapes from the vineyard for the poor and the stranger

Not stealing, lying, or double-dealing

Not taking false oaths

Paying workers their wages at the end of each working day

Not cursing the deaf or putting a stumbling block before a blind person

Not talebearing or gossiping

Not practicing prostitution

Respecting the aged

Keeping and using only honest weights, scales, and measures in business (Lev. 19)

These are very difficult, very demanding actions which are required for people to be holy. They are the yardsticks against which individuals can measure their activities. We usually think of holy people as unworldly individuals removed from society: monks, priests, or very pious people who live lonely or secluded lives. That, as you can see, is not what Judaism expects of people who wish to be holy. It expects people to relate to their fellow human beings honestly and fairly. It expects compassion and respect.

But what makes these values Jewish? Aren't these the kinds of standards that all people should be expected to follow, whether or not they are Jewish? Of course. There is nothing in either these ethical demands or those found elsewhere in our Torah that are reserved for Jews alone. Non-Jews also consider these values important standards for behavior. As a matter of fact, they are found in the codes of behavior of many other religious (and nonreligious) groups. At the same time, they are most closely associated with Jews and Judaism because our ancestors first gathered them together and wrote them down in what we call a religious code. They connected these values with their idea of God. And because they felt they were such important standards for human behavior, they said that God demands this of people.

These "demandments" were part of a pattern of doing, which the early Hebrew people called *mitzvot.* Thus, Jews were commanded to provide for the poor and the needy in the community by not harvesting the corners of the fields, so that the poor could come in and pick or gather without shame. This practice became known as doing a *mitzvah,* fulfilling a Divine commandment. Likewise, the observance of Shabbat or the festivals became a mitzvah.

The Jewish people gave their own unique expression to these values. Judaism became a very highly structured system of rules and regulations governing ethical conduct. All were connected to what was called God's will. Was it really God's will? No one knows for sure. Certainly it was what the leaders of the Jewish people believed God wanted. It was known as a covenant or contract between God and the Jewish people. God made certain promises to the Jewish people that God would fulfill if the people kept their end of the bargain by doing the mitzvot.

But how could these leaders of the Jewish people be so

sure that they knew what God wanted? Because they saw what helped and what hurt both individuals and the larger societies in which people lived! They wanted to make certain these values were preserved and followed, so they associated them with God. Historically, people give importance to an idea or a thing either by saying it is very old (as an antique) or by associating it with someone or something that is very respected. If somebody gives you a ring and tells you, "It was your great-grandmother's and it has been handed down in this family from mother to daughter for three generations," you are going to guard it a lot more carefully than if somebody gives you a ring and tells you, "I bought it for you last week at a garage sale. Be careful with it." Or, if someone tells you that she learned this or that from a professor or teacher with whom she had lunch last week, there is a greater possibility that you will accept what she tells you than if she said she heard it from some youngster at the neighborhood gas station. Age and experience usually (but not always) give authority. In Jewish tradition, God is the ultimate authority.

Who were the Jewish leaders?

You already know some of them pretty well: the patriarchs—Abraham, Isaac, and Jacob—and matriarchs—Sarah, Rebeccah, Rachel, and Leah—as well as such heroes and heroines as Joseph, Moses, Deborah, Jael, and Ruth. But there were others, too, who had a powerful impact on the life and thinking of the ancient Jewish community as well as on Jews throughout history. These were the prophets of Israel. We know a great deal about them. Much that they said and wrote has survived. Their teachings are called *Nevuah,* or prophecy. What they said, did, and wrote made a lot of sense, even though most of the people who lived during the prophets' lifetimes did not like them and ignored their teachings. The prophets were the greatest teachers of values the Jewish people ever had. Most of them lived lonely and tragic lives, rejected by their own people and respected only after their deaths when what they said came to be seen as lasting truths.

The standards they demanded of the people were and are the really important values of life, more important than fame, money, and success. That is why men and women of all religions, not only Judaism, still probe the prophets today for deeper meanings. If you want to know about values on which to build your life, you have to study the prophets of Israel. That is why we have chosen the prophets as a springboard for our exploration of values.

II

Who's Who among the Prophets

THERE were fifteen important prophets in Israel. Their careers covered nearly four centuries, beginning about 750 B.C.E. They make up the group we call the *literary prophets,* either because they wrote down their prophecies or because we have books in the Bible named after them. Seven of the fifteen were truly outstanding. In the order in which they lived they were: Amos, Hosea, Isaiah, Micah, Jeremiah, Ezekiel, and Deutero-(Second) Isaiah. Others—like Nathan, Elijah, and Elisha, who had characteristics of the prophets —lived earlier. A few like Haggai, Zechariah, and Malachi, lived a century later than the last of the seven prophets listed above. A few—Joel, Obadiah, Nahum, Habakkuk, and Zephaniah—lived, taught, and wrote their books between the times that Amos, Hosea, Isaiah, and Micah lived and the years when Jeremiah, Ezekiel, and Deutero-Isaiah dominated the scene. Before you get too mixed up, look at the charts at the front of the book. That will show you who's who among the prophets and when they prophesied.

WHAT IS A PROPHET?

The great literary prophets of Israel shared five basic characteristics. First, they were *solitary* figures. To use the language of our own day, they were "loners." They didn't travel in groups or have many close friends. While some— Hosea, Isaiah, and Jeremiah—were married and had families, even they remained separate from the rest of the community. They were involved in the affairs of their days, yes, but not as kings, priests, or politicians running for public office or interested in winning popularity contests. They were all quite unpopular, hated and denounced by many of the people whose lives they sought to change. Maybe that's one of the reasons they were not very effective in their own times.

A second characteristic of the prophets is that they were seen as *God's mouthpieces,* speaking for God. None of them really wanted to be prophets at first. None of them wanted the role that God thrust upon them, but not one seemed able to get away from the task. Read the Bible's account of how four of the greatest became prophets:

> A lion has roared,
> Who can but fear?
> My Lord God has spoken,
> Who can but prophesy?
>
> Amos 3:8

In the year that King Uzziah died, I beheld my Lord seated on a high and lofty throne; and the skirts of His robe filled the Temple. Seraphs stood in attendance on Him. Each of them had six wings: with two he covered his face, with two he covered his legs, and with two he would fly.

And one would call to the other,
"Holy, holy, holy!
The Lord of Hosts!
His presence fills all the earth!"
The doorposts would shake at the sound of the one who called, and the House kept filling with smoke. I cried,
"Woe is me; I am lost!
For I am a man of unclean lips
And I live among a people
Of unclean lips;
Yet my own eyes have beheld
The King Lord of Hosts."
Then one of the seraphs flew over to me with a live coal, which he had taken from the altar with a pair of tongs. He touched it to my lips and declared,

"Now that this has touched your lips,
Your guilt shall depart
And your sin be purged away."
Then I heard the voice of my Lord saying, "Whom shall I
send? Who will go for us?" And I said, "Here am I; send
me."

Isa. 6:1–8

The word of the Lord came to me:
Before I created you in the womb, I selected you;
Before you were born, I consecrated you;
I appointed you a prophet concerning the nations.

Jer. 1:4–5

And He said to me, "O mortal, stand up on your feet
that I may speak to you." As He spoke to me, a spirit
entered into me and set me upon my feet; and I heard
what was being spoken to me. He said to me, "O mortal,
I am sending you to the people of Israel, that nation of
rebels, who have rebelled against Me.—They as well as
their fathers have defied Me to this very day; for the sons
are brazen of face and stubborn of heart. I send you to
them, and you shall say to them: 'Thus said the Lord
God'—"

Ezek. 2:1–4

In each of these instances, the prophets were drafted into
God's service. Did God really speak to them? Or could it be
that what they heard was the voice of their own consciences,
something inside them demanding that they become prophets? That possibility is not as strange as it may seem. Have
you ever heard the voice of your own conscience disturbing
you, telling you to do something that you wish you didn't
have to do? Just imagine what that drive must be like in
adults who know that what is being asked is going to make
them very unpopular with their family, their community,
their community leader. It takes courage to say yes to that
call of conscience, especially if all around us others seem to
be saying no! The prophets didn't say yes easily either. They
did so only when the condition of the world in which they

lived became so oppressive that they could no lon[...] silent.

And that brings us to the third characteristic w[...] the literary prophets shared: They arose in times of social or political crisis in Israel. They prophesied in rel[...] to specific events that either had taken place or were about to occur. The prophet Nathan (who, while not considered one of the great literary prophets, did have all the qualities of a prophet) stood before King David (1000 B.C.E.) after the king had issued an order to have Uriah, the husband of Bathsheba, put into the battle line where he was sure to be killed. Nathan publicly accused King David of murder. "That man is you!" he thundered at David. Standing in David's throne room, he denounced the king as an adulterer and a murderer (2 Sam. 11–12).

Imagine Nathan's courage. Remember, David was an absolute monarch. He had the power of life and death in his hands. He could have ordered Nathan killed immediately and Nathan knew that, even as he knew that to accuse the king of Israel in public was to humiliate him. But to Nathan there were more important issues involved than his own life. If the king of Israel could commit murder because he was sexually attracted to another man's wife, and go unpunished, imagine the example that would set for the rest of the people! Such behavior could not go unchallenged; too much was at stake—the integrity of the family, the sacredness of marriage, and the laws against violence and bloodshed. If these values were violated, the welfare of society would be shattered. And so Nathan confronted King David at the risk of his own life and—believe it or not—David listened, accepted the judgment and repented. Even a king of Israel was accountable to God's judgment.

This incident illustrates a fourth characteristic of the prophets: their ability to *predict* what would happen to the people if they followed a certain course of action. The accuracy of their predictions was not grounded in some magical crystal ball gazing, reading horoscopes, or tarot cards.

The prophets were keen analysts of their times, and their conclusions were based on the clarity of their own intellectual insights. Even if those with whom they lived rejected the warnings, their words survived because, generations later, people could see that the prophets had spoken the truth.

They seemed to understand that all actions have consequences. Today we call it the principle of cause and effect. The prophets understood that, just as the natural law is governed by the laws of cause and effect, so too, in human nature, moral laws operate in the affairs of human beings. This, they saw, was true for society as well as for individuals. On the personal level, acts such as theft, violence, and murder generate their own effects: distrust, hatred, counter-killing. Similarly, when engaged in by large groups of people, such activities stimulate national distrust, group hatred, war, even as positive activities evoke positive responses.

The Hebrew prophets were the first in recorded history to discover the reality and the power of this moral law. Because they discerned and articulated this moral truth, the prophets have been immortalized and their words have spoken to all succeeding generations. History and human experience have shown that the beliefs they stood for are really important values that can keep us alive and fully human. That, too, is a major characteristic of prophecy.

Finally, the fifth characteristic is that the prophets were *literate*. Some wrote down their own words; others had scribes to whom they dictated their messages. Jeremiah had a scribe named Baruch who "wrote down in the scroll, at Jeremiah's dictation, all the words which the Lord had spoken to him" (Jer. 36:4). Habakkuk seems to suggest that God wanted the prophets to write their messages so that all could know clearly what the prophets were saying:

> The Lord answered me and said:
> Write the prophecy down,

Inscribe it clearly on tablets,
So that it can be read easily.

Hab. 2:2

They wrote with astounding skill and beauty. One reason why people throughout the ages continue to read and re-read the prophets is the beauty of their language. Their messages are poetic and majestic in their power and grandeur.

Is there no balm in Gilead,
Can no physician be found?
Why has healing not yet
Come to my poor people?
Oh, that my head were water,
My eyes a fount of tears!
Then would I weep day and night
For the slain of my poor people.

Oh, to be in the desert,
At an encampment for wayfarers!
Oh, to leave my people,
To go away from them—
For they are all adulterers,
A band of rogues.

They bend their tongues like bows;
They are valorous in the land
For treachery, not for honesty;
They advance from evil to evil.
And they do not heed Me

—declares the LORD.

Beware, every man of his friend!
Trust not even a brother!
For every brother takes advantage,
Every friend is base in his dealings.

Jer. 8:22–9:3

The prophets were the radicals of their age and, like most radicals, the things they said demanded too much from the people who heard them. Most of the people looked upon them as crazy and chose to ignore them. The prophets made the people uncomfortable, challenging them to do things that they didn't want to do, even if it may have been for their own good. It was a situation very much like today. We know, for example, that cigarette smoking is unhealthy, increases the possibility of lung cancer and even death. Yet, despite all the warnings, many people are smoking more than ever before. They seem either not to care or to have a self-destructive impulse.

We exhibit the same tendency on an international level. Everyone knows that a few nuclear bombs dropped on the earth could wipe out all of humanity. Yet every nation that can, rushes into developing nuclear weapons, each with many times the lethal force of the bombs which devastated Nagasaki and Hiroshima during World War II. Of course, each nation develops them in the name of self defense and national security, and swears it will not use them. But the bombs are there. The impulsive anger of some deranged national leader could cause him or her to press a fatal button. Besides, accidents can and do happen. Do you think the people of the world have a secret desire to commit international suicide? Or are we just afraid to change our ways? What would the prophets say about the insane spread of nuclear weaponry? And how would the public today react to the prophets?

THERE WERE PROPHETS BEFORE THERE WERE PROPHETS

Up to now we have described the characteristics of the great literary prophets of Israel. But, as you read the Bible and Jewish history, you will see that other figures were also referred to as prophets. Abraham was called a prophet: "But you must restore the man's wife—since he is a

prophet" (Gen. 20:7). Moses was called a prophet twice in
the Bible:

> The Lord your God will raise up for you a prophet from
> among your own people like myself; him you shall heed.
> Deut. 18:15

> Never again did there arise in Israel a prophet like Moses,
> whom the Lord singled out, face to face . . . .
> Deut. 34:10

Moses was a man who spoke for God in a special way, though
he was better known as a lawgiver and leader of the established community. The literary prophets, on the other hand,
were critics of the social order and seemed always to stand
outside the establishment.

In the Book of Judges, Gideon is referred to as a prophet
(6:8) and once Deborah is called a prophetess (Judg. 4:4).
Women's liberation came early in Jewish history!

VARIETIES OF PROPHETS

The word prophet has meant different things at different
times in Jewish history. A distinction has to be drawn between a false and a true prophet. In some instances both
were called *navi*. King Saul, for example, was a navi before
he became king of Israel. We are told that he would, on
occasion, join the bands of roving *nevi'im* who were well-
known for the wild ecstatic trances into which they would
fall. These people would work themselves into states of high
emotional frenzy, losing all contact with reality. The priest
Samuel knew that Saul participated in this kind of group.
Immediately after he anointed Saul the first king of Israel,
Samuel urged him to join with a band of the ecstatic nevi'im
and prophesy with them. (Read 1 Sam. 10:5–11.) Note in verse
11 that the people seemed to ridicule Saul for his behavior:

> When all who knew him previously saw him speaking in
> ecstasy together with the prophets, the people said to one
> another, "What's happened to the son of Kish? Is Saul too
> among the prophets?"
>
> 1 Sam. 10:11

In modern psychological language, Saul would probably be
described as a paranoid manic-depressive. And yet he was
the first king of Israel. Read 1 Samuel, chapters 7–16 and
18–19, and see if you can figure out why we describe him in
such harsh terms.

The bands of ecstatic prophets Saul often joined were
fairly common in ancient Israel. Elijah encountered them
on Mt. Carmel. They were priests of the false god Baal (see
1 Kings 18). Over and over again the Bible warns against
listening to them or following what they said:

> Let no one be found among you who consigns his son or
> daughter to the fire, or who is an augur, a soothsayer, a
> diviner, a sorcerer, one who casts spells, or one who con-
> sults ghosts or familiar spirits, or one who inquires of the
> dead.
>
> Deut. 18:10–11

There were also seers in ancient Israel, those who divined
the future through visions. These were not the literary
prophets.

> Formerly in Israel, when a man went to inquire of God,
> he would say, "Come, let us go to the seer," for the
> prophet of today was formerly called a seer.
>
> 1 Sam. 9:9

Occasionally the Bible used the words prophet and seer
interchangeably, and that makes the matter confusing to the
average reader:

When David rose in the morning, the word of the Lord
had come to the prophet Gad, David's seer.

2 Sam. 24:11

Gad was not a literary prophet. He was a diviner, a visionary
of sorts who, perhaps having some special power, appeared
to speak in God's name.

The nevi'im were the professional prophets whom the
kings of Israel would hire. They were kept in the court and
used to consult oracles or to make divinations. This was
especially important before a big military campaign. Once
King Ahab of Israel and Jehoshaphat of Judah used them
(1 Kings 22:1–23). Most of the professional prophets told the
kings what they wanted to hear, though a few were independent and quite courageous. Elijah's condemnation of
Ahab (1 Kings 21), Ahijah's involvement in the revolt against
Jeroboam (1 Kings 11:29–39), and Elisha's inspiration of the
successful revolt against Jehu (2 Kings 9) are all exciting
examples of this independence. Elijah particularly deserves
to be looked at a little more closely. Some people only think
of Elijah as a fanciful figure who flies all over the Jewish
world on *Pesach,* invisibly entering our homes through a
door opened for him, tasting from a special wine cup left out
for him on the Seder table. Moreover, they consider him to
be a forerunner of the Messiah.

Actually Elijah should be remembered for better and
different reasons. He was one of the very first who was willing to risk his life for what was to become a great theme of
the prophets, one of the ideas that has kept the Jewish people alive for over 2,000 years: ISRAEL IS NOT A NATION
LIKE ALL THE OTHERS. ISRAEL MUST BE A SPE-
CIALLY ETHICAL AND JUST PEOPLE. IT IS TO BE THE
BEARER OF A HIGHER IDEA, EXEMPLIFYING GOD'S
WILL ON EARTH.

Does this idea make you a little uncomfortable? Why?
This is the way it happened. A king by the name of Ahab

ruled the northern kingdom of Israel between the years 874–852 B.C.E. At that time Israel was weak. Assyria, a powerful empire north of Israel, exacted tribute from her tiny southern neighbor Israel. To the east, the kingdom of Damascus had just defeated Israel in battle. Ahab struggled to hold Israel together. He was a strong king. His one weakness was his love for his Phoenician wife, Jezebel. Her father had been a priest of the hated god Baal and was now king of Tyre, a foreign city in the north. To honor his wife (and perhaps also to keep peace between the two countries), Ahab had a temple built to Baal in the Israelite capital of Samaria. This was an intolerable act to Elijah. There could be no room for Baal or any other false god in Israel. In Israel, God alone was supreme. Elijah's opposition to Baal also became an opposition to Jezebel, the queen.

His hatred of this woman was reinforced by an affair involving the vineyard of a man named Naboth. Ahab wanted the vineyard of this poor man. When Naboth refused to sell it to the king, Queen Jezebel decided to make the resistance a test of the king's power. Under her command, Naboth was falsely accused of blasphemy and stoned to death. With a kind of contemptuous pride, she then presented the vineyard to her husband, the king. At the vineyard, Ahab was confronted by Elijah who, in a towering rage, denounced him and prophesied the disgraceful downfall of his kingdom (1 Kings 21).

Elijah did not announce the destruction of the ruling house on account of its idolatry, but because of the gross *injustice* it committed against one simple person. Again we see the actions of a king judged by the standards of God. Neither king nor people could expect to remain unpunished if they fell away from that standard of God's absolute morality. God's demands were as uncompromising as they were clear: *just* relations between people, honesty in action. No one, not even a king, could stand above the moral law. These were the tests by which to measure whether Israel was really the people of God. Long after Elijah, prophet after prophet continued to preach the same message. The failure of the people to live up to these standards was the reason given by later prophets for the tragedy of exile.

Now we have a better idea of what a prophet is and is not. We know a little more about the characteristics that distinguish a true literary prophet from others.

Have there been other prophets since those biblical days?

Was Mohammed a prophet? Was Jesus a prophet?

Muslims consider Mohammed to be a true prophet and some Christians believe that Jesus was one.

WAS JESUS A PROPHET?

The honest answer we can give to this difficult question is that, while some Christians think Jesus was a prophet in the great tradition of literary prophecy, Jews do not. Jesus lived 500 years after the death of the prophet Malachi (ca. 516 B.C.E.), the last of the literary prophets. Jesus may have rejected the designation of prophet for himself, preferring instead to let some think of him as divine. The New Testament suggests this:

> Now when Jesus came into the district of Caesarea Philippi, he asked his disciples, "Who do men say the Son of man is?" And they said, "Some say John the Baptist, others say Elijah, and others Jeremiah or one of the prophets." He said to them, But who do you say that I am?" Simon Peter replied, "You are the Christ, the Son of the living God." And Jesus answered him, "Blessed are you, Simon Bar-Jona! For flesh and blood has not revealed this to you, but my Father who is in heaven."
>
> Matt. 16:13–17
> (Also see Mark 3:11–12)

No prophet ever made such a claim or permitted others so to think of him. In doing so, Jesus broke with a long and clearly established biblical tradition that no human being could ever be divine. While prophecy was a lonely calling, prophets were not isolated from their past. All felt themselves to be links in a succession of other prophets living within a tradition.

> . . . from the day your fathers left the land of Egypt until today . . . I kept sending all My servants, the prophets, to them daily and persistently, . . .
>
> Jer. 7:25

The prophets regarded each word they received and spoke as a continuation of a claim shared with earlier prophets.

Jesus' death was more important than his life. The prophets of Israel viewed their task as helping the people to free themselves from the oppression of stronger nations. Jesus saw his life as one which, *through his death,* would redeem all humankind from sin. Thus, his death became far more important than his life. His followers, and those who later wrote about him, portrayed Jesus as believing that he was born for the express purpose of dying in order to redeem humankind.

There are some modern Christians who have difficulty with the idea of Jesus' divinity. They emphasize the nobility and gentleness of his life. They speak of his unique capacity to understand life and teach about it. In their viewpoint, these qualities "establish him as a foremost man of all time, indeed, a person after whom modern people can model themselves."* Jews should have no difficulty understanding the great humanity of Jesus. He was, after all, a Jew, not a Christian, to the very end of his life. He became central to Christianity and, for some Christians, he was considered a

---

*Samuel Sandmel, *A Little Book on Religion* (for people who are not religious) (Chambersburg, Pennsylvania: Wilson Books, 1975), p. 137.

prophet—not because he was a great ethical teacher, but because he was viewed as divine, the Christ. They revered him as a divine being who had temporarily become a man when he appeared on this earth and who, through his death, sought to redeem humankind. Jews accept the humanity of Jesus, not the divinity of Christ.

The literary prophets were ethical geniuses. They discovered and expressed basic moral truths. They were not really teachers. Teachers transmit to their students what they have learned from others. Jesus was more of a teacher than a prophet. He was, by his life, a superb role-model but not a particularly original thinker. He lived a nobly ethical life, but he did not create a set of ethics new or different from the Jewish ethics of his day, which he learned from his teachers. They, in turn, inherited what they taught from the prophets.

There are some who believe that new prophets have arisen in the twenty-five centuries since the close of the prophetic period. Some consider people like Karl Marx, Mahatma Gandhi, and Martin Luther King, Jr., to have been prophets in their days, though these men never called themselves prophets in the biblical sense. During the 1960s in the United States, many young people even looked upon the Beatles, Joan Baez, or Bob Dylan as prophetic because of the radical and socially demanding things they said in their music. However, none of these persons met the basic requirements of true prophecy. They cannot be considered prophets in the biblical sense, even though they seem to share certain characteristics associated with the great prophets. As the literary prophets mixed politics and religion, involving themselves in political controversy and sometimes demonstrating against policies they thought were wrong, so too did those modern people to whom we have referred. As the prophets arose in times of social crisis, so do those who speak out in more contemporary times. In fact, in almost every way except one, they fit the definition of a literary prophet. And that exception is critical: *They did*

*not consider themselves chosen by God to speak for God.
They never represented themselves as speaking in God's
name.* They surely thought they were right, and on God's
side, perhaps—but speaking for God? No!

Sometimes, personalities connected with a religious
movement, like priests, ministers, or rabbis, are called prophetic. That is often because they take courageous social
stands and do so in the name of their religious traditions,
often identifying their stands with those taken earlier by the
prophets. In these instances, however, they are *interpreting*
the prophets, not viewing themselves as prophets. They
may be dedicated servants of God as they understand God.
They may seek to reform their churches and synagogues.
They may demand that the people of their religious communities change their ways. They may even put their bodies
on the line for their beliefs, as did many clergy and religious
lay leaders who have gone to jail for justice during the Civil
Rights movement in this country, in protest against war, for
the rights of labor, or for the defense of civil liberties. But
they were not prophets as we use that term.

CAN YOU OR I BE A PROPHET?

Not in the traditional meaning of that word. But this does
not mean that we have no prophetic role today. It is never
out of season or futile for an individual to stand against
wrong when he or she sees it.

There is a talmudic story that describes a great rabbi,
Sussya, crying desolately before his death. "Why are you
crying, Master?" his disciples asked him. "I am crying," he
said, "not because I did not measure up to Moses, or to
Isaiah, or to Jacob. I am crying because I didn't fully measure
up to *Sussya!*"

That is the real message of the prophets. We cannot be
an Isaiah or an Amos. But we can be, fully and completely,
the best that is in each of us to be. The prophets didn't just

tell other people what to do and how to live. They practiced what they preached. Their own lives were proof of their teachings. The prophets were true models, because they were whole persons. The struggle to refine the world is a desperately important one, but it starts inside each human heart. No struggle is as anguished and hard as is the struggle by each person to be worthy of the calling as a child of God, a human being, a living and caring person in a changing world.

III

Truth(and Consequences)

HAVE you ever thought what it might be like to be obliged to tell only the truth for 24 hours? Many have tried and failed. Some have gotten themselves into trouble in the effort.

Everyone knows the story of Pinocchio, whose nose grew every time he lied until it became grotesque. One social psychologist in the United States recently estimated that the average American outstrips Pinocchio by telling as many as 200 lies a day (including white lies and false excuses). Lying has become a serious problem of major proportions.

A young friend of ours, whom we will call Josh, decided he would try to be a total truth-teller for one full day. His day, as he reported it to us later, went something like this:

Josh came to breakfast and his mother asked, "You finished your homework last night, didn't you?" "No," said Josh. At that moment, Josh's older sister, Abigail, swept into the room showing off a new dress she planned to wear to school. "Morning, Josh. How do you like my dress?" Josh swallowed hard, remembered his promise to himself, and said, "Terrible, like something the cat dragged in."

Josh's mother was astonished. "How could you say such a thing to your sister?" she demanded. "It's the truth," he answered. "Isn't that what you want?" All that day it was the same thing. Josh told his teacher that he was the most boring teacher Josh had. He told Helen, the girl in the next seat in his homeroom, that she needed deodorant. At dinner, he told his mother that her lasagna tasted like rubber. When his father shouted at him for his rudeness, Josh said: "You don't like to hear the truth. And you holler too much. And that's the truth!"

Josh's day of truth-telling was memorable. The family still talks about it. But it makes you think. Is it always right to tell the truth? Is telling the truth the only value? What about not hurting other people's feelings? What if telling the truth conflicts with the value of not doing to others what you wouldn't want done to you? People often get into trouble when they try to tell others the whole truth, even if it is for their own good.

A few years ago, a young man named Ralph Nader began to campaign for automobile safety. He warned the public that more people had been killed by automobiles than had died in all the wars in American history. And he proved that many of those deaths could have been avoided if automobile manufacturers cared less about big cars and flashy features, and a little more about safety. The public ignored Nader. But Nader quietly gathered the facts and published a hard-hitting book entitled *Unsafe at Any Speed*. The auto manufacturers, instead of facing the truth of his evidence, set out to destroy his reputation. General Motors hired detectives to investigate Nader's private life. They circulated rumors about his sex life and his emotional health. But these tactics backfired. Nader sued General Motors for harassment. The case was settled out of court, and General Motors paid Nader over $400,000 in damages. The furor this kicked up finally made Congress face the truth. They passed a law making safety belts compulsory in every new car, and set other standards for minimum safety. Truth usually wins out in the long run, but often the truth-tellers endure a great deal of abuse.

Is there a difference between a lie and a fib? Yes. Most people believe this, and on frequent occasions fib a little, usually to protect someone's feelings. An argument might be made for fibbing to protect someone else's feelings. Kindness, too, is a value, as is truth-telling. Weighing these two values against one another, sometimes it is more *value*-able to choose kindness.

What about passive lying—remaining silent when you see a wrong being committed, or when you know that by not keeping silent you can effect a positive good?

In your class in public school your teacher announces one day that some cocaine has been found in an envelope in the back of the room. She asks the person responsible, or anyone who knows who is responsible, to see her privately after school. You know the person who brought the drug into class. What should you do? Do you tell the truth or do you keep silent, feeling that it is wrong to inform on someone?

Edmund Burke, a very smart English politician who lived during the eighteenth century, once wrote: "The only thing necessary for the triumph of evil is for good [people] to do nothing." How does such a thought affect your attitude toward informing?

Truth-telling is difficult for all of us, because it usually runs into conflict with other values. In this case, truth collides with the value of personal popularity. Imagine how unpopular a student would be with other students if they found out who "ratted" to the teacher. But if what was at stake was the value of student morale, or school reputation, or the existence of a condition in the classroom where learning became impossible, then what? What if truth conflicted with so important a value as the law of the land?

BLOWING THE WHISTLE

The movie *Jaws* portrayed an important ethical dilemma. When the local sheriff realized that a carnivorous shark was endangering the seashore community, the community's business and civic leaders pressured him to keep the truth to himself, because publicity would ruin business and deprive hundreds of townsfolk of their livelihood. Did the sheriff have a moral duty to blow the whistle?

The United States government constantly faces the same dilemma. You may remember when tests on mice indicated that saccharine could cause cancer. It was not certain that it would affect human beings, except if taken in extremely large doses. But neither could the authorities be certain that it would not harm human beings. Should the Food and Drug Administration have published a warning on the use of saccharine, as is done with cigarettes? The argument against a warning was that it could wipe out an entire industry and cause serious economic harm to many people. The F.D.A. decided to blow the whistle. Were they right to do so? Do we value the whistle-blowers, or do we tend to vilify them for disturbing the even tenor of our lives?

The examples of truth-telling we have drawn so far from the prophets Amos, Jeremiah, Isaiah, Ezekiel, and Habakkuk all share one thing in common: they are based upon the prophets' judgments against the people in hope that the people, seeing their faults, would change their behavior. The prophets did not wish to see Israel destroyed nor to harm the people. It was a desire to refine, not to destroy. This is the role of criticism in the truest sense; to point out what is wrong without malice. The real critic is a person who has deep positive feelings of affection for the object of the criticism.

In the nineteenth century, a famous Scandinavian playwright by the name of Henrik Ibsen wrote a play entitled *An Enemy of the People* which exemplified this attitude and the consequences of expressing it. The play takes place in a small Scandinavian resort known for its mineral springs. Tourists come from great distances to bathe in the waters, hoping for relief from their ailments. As the play opens, a local doctor makes a startling discovery: the waters are polluted.

The doctor's suspicions are aroused when several visitors contract typhoid and gastric fever. The doctor's alarm mounts as lab tests confirm his fears. Warning the town officials that the town faces the danger of a typhoid emergency, he demands that visitors should be told not to bathe in the mineral springs. Shocked, the mayor and his colleagues insist that the matter be hushed up: the tourist trade could be finished by such rumors. By the time new sewers could be made and water pipes corrected, visitors would have gone elsewhere and the town would be ruined. Anyway, only a few people had become sick so far. The doctor must be overreacting.

Pressure mounts as the doctor's close friends urge him not to release the lab data. He persists. When he goes to the local newspaper, the editor refuses to print the story. When the issue comes before a town meeting, the entire community turns on the doctor, shouting that his facts are a slander against the community. The play ends with neighbors gathered into a violent mob around the doctor's home, shouting curses and throwing rocks through the windows.

THE PAINFUL TRUTH

The prophets of Israel also had to make the terrible choice between telling the people the truth about what they saw, or submitting to the will of their kings and thus abiding by the law of the land. While we know the course of action they chose, it wasn't easy for them. They knew that the truth would hurt, and that people then, as now, would not welcome harsh truths. Some of them tried to beg off. The biblical character Jonah, for example, tried to run away altogether, coming very close to jumping ship.

Amos had to experience three visions of the impending destruction of the northern kingdom of Israel before he could be persuaded by God to respond to God's command to "Go, prophesy to My people Israel" (Amos 7:15).

None of these people enjoyed the role of truth-tellers.

They knew it would bring pain and rejection, and they were right. Jeremiah, for example, despaired at the words of condemnation he had to speak:

> Why must my pain be endless,
> My wound incurable,
> Resistant to healing?
> You have been to me like a spring that fails,
> Like waters that cannot be relied on.
>
> Jer. 15:18

He felt betrayed by God, whom he compared to a "deceitful brook," and he suffered terribly at the hands of the rulers who viewed his prophecies, which predicted the destruction of Judah, as nothing short of treason. Once a priest flogged him and put him in a cell (Jer. 20:2). Jeremiah did not cease to prophesy, but he complained bitterly to God. God, he cried, had deceived him and made him a laughingstock whom everyone mocked:

> For every time I speak, I must cry out,
> Must shout, "Lawlessness and rapine!"
> For the word of the Lord causes me
> Constant disgrace and contempt.
>
> Jer. 20:8

He cursed the day he was born (Jer. 15:10). But he continued to tell God's truth to the people: they would be led away captive to Babylon. On one occasion, a powerful group of priests and false prophets (those hired by King Jehoiakim to tell him what he wanted to hear) threatened to kill Jeremiah (see chapter 26). Finally, as an old man, seeing that the capture of Judah by Babylon was inevitable, he urged the people to ignore their king and submit to the Babylonians. For this he was falsely accused of being a deserter (Jer. 37: 11–15), thrown into a dungeon, and then into a cistern filled with slimy mud, where he was left to die of starvation (Jer.

38:6). Fortunately, he was saved by a servant in the king's house. Of course, all that he prophesied came true. On the ninth day of Av in the year 586 B.C.E., the Babylonian battering rams finally broke through the walls of the city of Jerusalem. The people were taken captive, and the sovereign state of Judah came to an end. But Jeremiah had also predicted that this terrible moment would not permanently end the Jewish presence in Israel. He prophesied the eventual end of the exile and the return of the people. He was right about that, too.

Jeremiah spoke the truth to the people all his life and paid a terrible price for his honesty. Up to his last days in Egypt, where he fled with a small group of refugees from Jerusalem, he tried to warn the people against idolatry and immoral behavior. He died as a martyr to the truth.

The lives of other prophets were similar. Amos challenged both the High Priest Amaziah and Jeroboam II, one of the most powerful kings the northern kingdom of Israel ever had. Amos challenged them in full view of all the people on New Year's Day, and he spoke out at Bethel, the nation's most important shrine (Bethel, in Samaria, was a strong northern city). Tens of thousands of people were gathered there to celebrate the day of the Lord, congratulating themselves for having merited God's special protection. This period in Israel's history was a prosperous time. The enemies of Israel had been beaten back. The king had expanded the borders of the country. Naturally, the people thought they must be doing something right and had come to Bethel to celebrate with lavish sacrifices, games, dances, and mock piety. Amos, a roughly dressed, wild-looking man, appeared as if from nowhere to challenge their assumptions and their pride:

> Ah, you who wish
> For the day of the Lord!
> Why should you want

The day of the Lord?
It shall be darkness, not light!
Surely the day of the Lord shall be
Not light, but darkness,
Blackest night without a glimmer.

Amos 5:18, 20

Ah, you who are at ease in Zion
And confident on the hill of Samaria,
You notables of the leading nation
On whom the House of Israel pin their hopes.

Amos 6:1

For I have noted how many are your crimes,
And how countless your sins—
You enemies of the righteous,
You takers of bribes,
You who subvert in the gate
The cause of the needy!

Assuredly,
At such a time the prudent man keeps silent,
For it is an evil time.

Amos 5:12–13

Imagine the reaction! Here was a total stranger, not even from their own country. Amos was a southerner, from Tekoa, a small town in the hill country south of Jerusalem. He not only attacked the people's self-righteous assumptions, he told them that their king would be killed and they would be destroyed and taken away captive.

For Amos has said, "Jeroboam shall die by the sword, and Israel shall be exiled from its soil."

Amos 7:11

If Amos had tried to select a way to become instantly hated, he couldn't have found one better. The reaction to his appearance was quite predictable. He was thrown out:

Amaziah also said to Amos, "Seer, off with you to the land
of Judah! Earn your living there, and do your prophesying
there. But don't ever prophesy again at Bethel; for it is a
king's sanctuary and a royal palace."

Amos 7:12–13

But Amos was to have the last word, in more ways than one.
First, he corrected the high priest:

Amos answered Amaziah: "I am not a prophet, and I am
not a prophet's disciple."

Amos 7:14

Amos means that he is not a professional prophet. He is not
one of those types with whom Saul, the first king, used to
cavort.

I am a cattle breeder and a tender of sycamore figs. But the
Lord took me away from following the flock, and the Lord
said to me, "Go, prophesy to My people Israel."

Amos 7:14–15

. . . but this, I swear, is what the Lord said: Your wife shall
play the harlot in the town, your sons and daughters shall
fall by the sword, and your land shall be divided up with
a measuring line. And you yourself shall die on unclean soil;
for Israel shall be exiled from its soil.

Amos 7:17

I will turn your festivals into mourning
And all your songs into dirges;
I will put sackcloth on all loins
And tonsures on every head.
I will make it mourn as for an only child,
All of it as on a bitter day.

Amos 8:10

A time is coming—declares my Lord God—when I will
send a famine upon the land: not a hunger for bread or a
thirst for water, but for hearing the words of the Lord. Men

shall wander from sea to sea and from north to east to seek
the word of the Lord, but they shall not find it.

Amos 8:1–12

Amos was never heard from again. But everything he
prophesied came true. In the year 721 B.C.E., less than
25 years after Amos spoke, the Assyrians (a great military power to the north of Israel) swept down on that
little kingdom, destroyed its cities and shrines, and took the
people captive.

Isaiah, Hosea, and Micah, contemporaries of Amos who
also lived immediately before the fall of the northern kingdom, experienced the same fates.

Hosea was not as hard on the people as was Amos. He
begged them to change their ways and their behavior. He
saw the rottenness of the way the people lived:

> Hear the word of the Lord,
> O people of Israel!
> For the Lord has a case
> Against the inhabitants of this land,
> Because there is no honesty and no goodness
> And no obedience to God in the land.
> False swearing, dishonesty, and murder,
> And theft and adultery are rife;
> Crime follows upon crime!

Hos. 4:1–2

> I will not punish their daughters for fornicating
> Nor their daughters-in-law for committing adultery;
> For they themselves turn aside with whores
> And sacrifice with prostitutes,
> And a people that is without sense must stumble.

Hos. 4:14

> They have made kings,
> But not with My sanction;
> They have made officers,
> But not of My choice.
> Of their silver and gold

They have made themselves images,
To their own undoing.

Hos. 8:4

When they present sacrifices to Me,
It is but flesh for them to eat:
The Lord has not accepted them.
Behold, He remembers their iniquity,
He will punish their sins:
Back to Egypt with them!

Hos. 8:13

You have plowed wickedness,
You have reaped iniquity—
And you shall eat the fruits of treachery—
Because you relied on your way,
On your host of warriors.

Hos. 10:13

Hosea uses a phrase which has become one of the most popular and most quoted lines of all prophetic writings:

They sow wind,
And they shall reap whirlwind—

Hos. 8:7

Hosea spoke the truth courageously, honestly, and painfully. But unlike Amos, Hosea did see the possibility of a future for the people. If they changed their behavior, they could survive, because God loves His people. They were like His children and no father wants to see his children destroyed:

I fell in love with Israel
When he was still a child;
And I have called him My son

Ever since Egypt.
I have pampered Ephraim,*

*Ephraim was one of the northern tribes. Hosea uses the name here as a symbol for all of Israel.

Taking them in My arms;
But they have ignored
My healing care.

Hos. 11:1,3

How can I give you up, O Ephraim?
How surrender you, O Israel?
How can I make you like Admah,
Render you like Zeboiim?
I have had a change of heart,
All My tenderness is stirred.

Hos. 11:8

As one reads these lines, one can begin to understand the suffering Hosea experienced as he prophesied dread events he saw coming. As God was in distress at the prospect of Israel's future, so was the prophet for he, too, loved his people and could not bear to think of what would happen to them. And so, he begged them to change, reassuring them that if they did, God would not permit their destruction:

Ephraim shall say:
"What more have I to do with idols?
When I respond and look to Him
I become like a verdant cypress."
Your fruit is provided by Me.

Hos. 14:9

Return, O Israel, to the Lord your God,
For you have fallen because of your sin.

Hos. 14:2

I will not act on My wrath,
Will not turn to destroy Ephraim.
For I am God, not man,
The Holy One in your midst:
I will not come in fury.

Hos. 11:9

The people paid no attention to Hosea. And they suffered the consequences.

Micah, too, was deeply disturbed by the truth he had to tell:

> My people!
> What wrong have I done you?
> What hardship have I caused you?
> Testify against Me.

Mic. 6:3

But there was no answer. The child (Judah) continued to treat the parent (God) with contempt:

> For son spurns father,
> Daughter rises up against mother,
> Daughter-in-law against mother-in-law—
> A man's own household
> Are his enemies.

Mic. 7:6

> They covet fields, and seize them;
> Houses, and take them away.
> They defraud men of their homes,
> And people of their land.

Mic. 2:2

With all his heart, Micah yearned for a change, for a better time. He dreamt of it:

> In the days to come,
> The Mount of the Lord's House shall stand
> Firm above the mountains;
> And it shall tower above the hills.
> The peoples shall gaze on it with joy,
> And the many nations shall go and shall say:
> "Come,
> Let us go up to the Mount of the Lord,
> To the House of the God of Jacob;
> That He may instruct us in His ways,

And that we may walk in His paths."
For instruction shall come forth from Zion,
The word of the Lord from Jerusalem.
Thus He will judge among the many peoples,
And arbitrate for the multitude of nations,
However distant;
And they shall beat their swords into plowshares
And their spears into pruning hooks.
Nation shall not take up
Sword against nation;
They shall never again know war;
But every man shall sit
Under his grapevine or fig tree
With no one to disturb him.
For it was the Lord of Hosts who spoke.

                                        Mic. 4:1–4

The people did not listen.

Of all the prophets of ancient Israel, Isaiah was perhaps the most fascinating, and the most difficult to accept. He prophesied for 40 years, from 740 B.C.E. to 700 B.C.E., when the mighty King Sennacherib of Assyria returned to his capital, there to be killed by his own sons (2 Kings 19:35–37). At one point in his prophetic career Isaiah was so saddened by what he saw happening, and so discouraged by the fact that no one listened to him, that he withdrew from public life (Isa. 8:16–18). He was ignored because he spoke truths that the people did not want to hear. Like his predecessor, Amos, and his contemporaries, Hosea and Micah, Isaiah tried to warn the people that their behavior would cause the destruction of their society and their nation.

"How dare you crush My people
And grind the faces of the poor?"
                          —says my Lord God of Hosts
                                        Isa. 3:15

The Lord said:
"Because the daughters of Zion
Are so vain

And walk with heads thrown back,
With roving eyes,
And with mincing gait,
Making a tinkling with their feet."

Isa. 3:16

Ah,
Those who add house to house
And join field to field
Till there is room for none but you
To dwell in the land!

Isa. 5:8

Ah,
Those who chase liquor
From early in the morning,
And till late in the evening
Are inflamed by wine!

Isa. 5:11

Imagine someone talking like that to an unscrupulous real estate agent, or walking into a local pub to criticize the patrons standing at the bar? The intruder would be thrown out. Nor would it occur to either of the parties being addressed that maybe the speaker had a point worth listening to.

The greater and more difficult truth that Isaiah addressed to king and people alike was the truth that what was to happen to the people of Judah was in God's hands. Isaiah really believed that God directed the fate and future of Judah. Because of this fierce conviction, he advised the king, Ahaz, to avoid political or military alliances with any other nation to save Judah from destruction or captivity. The king brushed aside the prophet's advice and paid a disastrous price for his mistake. The Assyrian empire to the north made Judah a slave state, and Ahaz ordered an Assyrian altar built in the temple in Jerusalem. To Isaiah, this act was final proof of the faithlessness for which his people would suffer even more terrible consequences. His words of warning, which he knew were words of truth, had fallen on deaf ears. All the signs that he had given to the king that made the truth visible had been held up before blind eyes. Isaiah was so discouraged that he stopped prophesying and withdrew from the community.

> So I will wait for the Lord, who is hiding His face from the House of Jacob, and I will trust in Him.
>
> Isa. 8:17

The prophecies that are found in chapters 28–33 of Isaiah deal primarily with this period and show how clearly and how passionately the prophet tried to show both king and people that such a gamble would prove itself to be a disaster! His warnings were not only based on his political ideas that a revolt against so strong a power as Assyria would boomerang. They flowed from his religious belief that God controlled history and that Assyria was an instrument in God's hands to punish the people of Judah (and Israel) for their faithlessness.

> Ha!
> Assyria, rod of My anger,
> In whose hand, as a staff, is My fury!
> I send him against an ungodly nation,
> I charge him against a people that provokes Me,
> To take its spoil and to seize its booty
> And to make it a thing trampled
> Like the mire of the streets.
>
> Isa. 10:5,6

The prophets exclaimed their deep beliefs, which they projected as truths. Beliefs are different from facts, although both may be true. It was a truth-fact that militarily Assyria was stronger than Judah, Egypt, or Babylon, or even the three in combination. It was a truth-belief (that is, a belief held by the speaker) that Assyria was God's instrument.

Only a fool rejects truth-fact. But even wise people some-times fail to agree on the importance of truth-beliefs. In-deed, beliefs projected as truths may or may not be fact. For example, the belief, stated by millions as a truth, that the Torah was written completely by God and given intact on Mount Sinai to Moses is an idea which may or may not be a fact. Or the beliefs, projected as truth, that people go to heaven or hell when they die, or that they will live again when the Messiah comes, or that God dwells in heaven, may or may not be facts. These are powerful religious ideas that millions of people accept and believe as truths. These beliefs greatly influence the way people live their lives. Millions of people live as though these things were true. Does that prove that they *are* true? It certainly does prove that they are important because they change so many lives.

So far we have examined the differences between fibs and lies. We have discussed the importance of truth-telling, particularly when the lives and welfare of others are at stake, as well as the pain that truth-telling often brings to the one who cannot keep silent. All these situations have been based on the idea that the truths in question were indeed real truths, the facts of which could not be disputed. Now, however, we are moving into a less clear area.

What if there is some question about the nature of the truth? After all, people can believe anything they want and project it as truth. There are some people who believe that the devil is as real and as powerful as God. Some even form groups called covens where, with weird rituals, they express this particular belief in worship forms. Some time ago, New Yorkers were shocked to read that the police discovered a man dead of cancer for two months, whose remains were being kept in an apartment on the West Side of New York City by a group of his friends. They stood vigil in front of his body for 24 hours a day waiting for him to return to life. It seems that this man in his lifetime had convinced his friends that he could perform miracles and would return to life in a different form.

During any year you are bound to read in the newspapers how groups, believing that the world is coming to an end on a specific day, leave their homes and go into the mountains to wait for what they call the final judgment day. Of course, when it doesn't happen, they say that their calculations must have been off, and they return to their homes and possessions (which, interestingly enough, they didn't sell or give away). They withdraw for a while to wait for the next Armageddon, the next moment the world is supposed to come to an end. Oh yes, one can project any belief as a truth. But how can we know when a truth-belief is really true, to be accepted and followed, and when it is just one person's notion?

The prophets taught that pursuing justice is necessary for the survival of society. Is that truth? Observe what happens if and when people do *not* try to be just. Sometimes for a while they seem to succeed. But what happens to society in the long run if people do not try to be just in their relationships with one another? What happens to a society where neighbors do not care about one another? Does the society become better or worse if these truths are ignored? Human experience, which is merely a way of saying what people have observed about human behavior over many thousands of years, confirms the truth of these values. The experience of an individual may indicate that injustice or stealing is profitable, or brings success. But if all people acted in these ways all the time, it would not take long for society to collapse. The truth of truth-beliefs is proved by the test of time. But is time the only test?

We have suggested that there are some beliefs that people have held for long periods of time which we think are not true, such as the belief that the Bible was given completely to Moses on Mt. Sinai. Don't these beliefs indicate that the test of observation and experience is at best limited, even faulty? No, not necessarily. Human knowledge about these matters, accumulated over the course of time, has added strength to our reasons for rejecting these beliefs as untrue convictions. More and more people now know that the Bible came into existence over the course of hundreds of years and was written by many different people.

Similarly, more and more people have grown skeptical about the truth of resurrection or the belief in heaven or hell as actual places. Nevertheless, there is what one American thinker once described as "the will to believe." Sometimes people want to believe things they know are not factually true because it makes them more comfortable, or gives them hope. Besides, the challenges of modern knowledge to some of these convictions has caused many of those who hold them to develop an entire thought process by which to interpret or to explain the beliefs they have inherited. This process of interpretation helps them save the ideas they may not yet be ready to throw away. When Isaiah spoke of Assyria as "the rod of God," he was not projecting a false truth-conviction. Neither was he building a web of interpretation around his "will to believe." He truly believed it. However, his conviction that God has a hand in what happens to a people, that God is God of history, is a truth-belief, not a truth-fact, and is as difficult for people to accept now as it was then. What happened to the people of Judah seemed to confirm his belief. As we look back and see what happened, it can be said that he spoke the truth.

Isaiah's conviction that God controls the destiny of people and nations is powerfully expressed in an image. When God is finished using Assyria, said Isaiah, God will overthrow that nation. Therefore let not Assyria become too proud, thinking that it is its own power that enables it to punish Israel. Assyria is compared to an axe, with God as the one who wields it.

> Does an ax boast over him who hews with it,
> Or a saw magnify itself above him who wields it?
> As though the rod swung him who lifts it,
> As though the staff lifted the man!
>
> Isa. 10:15

The Lord of Hosts has sworn this oath:
"As I have designed, so shall it happen;
What I have planned, that shall come to pass:
To break Assyria in My land,
To crush him on My mountain."
And his yoke shall drop off them,
And his burden shall drop from their backs.

Isa. 14:24–25

People of faith should submit not to the Assyrian power, but to the power of God. They should understand God's judgment against them for the social wrongs of which they have been guilty, and they should wait patiently for the time when God will also cut down the aggressor nation, which He is only using now for His own purposes.

Would you expect a king or people to accept such a prophecy? No? Neither did Isaiah. And so he began to speak of only a remnant, a small part of the people who would understand and be left alive to continue the Jewish people.

And the survivors of the House of Judah that have escaped
shall renew its trunk below and produce boughs above.
For a remnant shall come forth from Jerusalem,
Survivors from Mount Zion.
The zeal of the Lord of Hosts
Shall bring this to pass.

Isa. 37:31–32

No one can talk about the fearless truth-telling of the prophets of Israel without recognizing that there was something special about them which they all shared in common: the fact that they seemed *compelled*, sometimes even against their will, to speak out in the face of the most difficult circumstances. They spoke the truth because they were, as we have pointed out earlier, the mouthpieces of God. They spoke God's words in God's name.

Most of us do not claim to have heard the voice of God. Can we nonetheless stick to truth? When the net of lies is all about us—in our television, our advertising, our politics, the dealings of our nations—can we still be truthful?

Time magazine (April 3, 1978) described a survey which showed that 69 percent of the public now believes that the nation's leaders have consistently lied to them over the past 10 years. Should certain kinds of lies be permitted, or is lying always wrong? Should a doctor be permitted, or expected, to give a placebo to a patient? Should police use unmarked cruisers? One answer to this question is that those lies may be permissible if and when they are known and approved in advance by the general public. Others would answer differently.

The trouble with small, innocent lies is not only that they violate the truth; it is also that small deceits may add up to a habit. People learn to deceive. We deceive ourselves. A lifetime of deceit puts masks on people, and we are no longer ourselves—we become actors playing a role. Such people grow up as adults who, out of habit, resort to deceit. They deceive their mates; they do not level with their children. When enough people live lives of deceit, they spawn corrupt politicians, corrupt police, and corrupt government policies. The prophets sensed this, which is why they decried even small falsehoods. Lying and half-truths seem trivial to the person telling them. But lying can corrupt a nation —think of Watergate, and Vietnam. This is part of our national problem today. If our leaders lie to us sometimes, we may not believe them *any* of the time. Lying kills trust; it creates a world of distrust, of locks, fences, walls—a jungle.

Jewish teaching has always stressed the terrible damage that lies—and gossip—can cause. Stealing a person's reputation, through lying or gossip, was always regarded as just as bad as stealing property. "You shall not render an unfair decision: do not favor the poor or show deference to the rich; judge your neighbor fairly. Do not deal basely with your fellows. Do not profit by the blood of your neighbor: I am the Lord" (Lev. 19:15,16) was a stern rule of Jewish law. There have been vulgar politicians in American life who have gone up and down the land spreading slander about innocent people. Hitler held power in Germany by lying about Jews and others. His belief was that no matter how big the lie ("Jews control the world," for example), if it were repeated often enough, people would believe it!

TRUTH IN MODERN GOVERNMENT

There are some people who say that it is perfectly all right for a government to tell lies to other governments. For example, we could not be expected to tell the Russians (or any other potential enemy) where all our bombs and missiles are placed, or where our nuclear submarines operate. But if it is all right to keep the truth from a foreign government, does the government have a right to lie to its own citizens? Some of the Arab governments have made it a practice to tell lies to their own people about the State of Israel. The Soviet Union prints vicious stories in newspapers about Jewish people (and about Israel), which everyone knows are lies. For example, because Communism is against religion, Russian newspapers often tell frightening stories about the supposed drunkenness and thievery which they say goes on in the synagogue. These are obvious untruths. They are anti-Semitic lies.

But even in free countries like the United States, the government is not always honest with its citizens. During the Vietnam War, for example, leaders of the government hid important events. One terrible example is the American massacre of Vietnam civilians at My Lai. For over a year the truth about this tragic event was known to many government leaders, who kept it quiet in the hope that it would not become public knowledge. Finally, a stubborn and brave-hearted journalist named Seymour Hersh pursued the story and brought out the facts. There were many Americans who were very angry when this became known. Some of them blamed Mr. Hersh, the newspapers, and the television networks which carried the story. Is it possible that sometimes the truth should not be told, that it is just too painful or hurtful to bear, that the results are even worse than keeping the truth hidden? What do you think? Some say that people always hate the messenger who brings unpleasant truth. The reporter Seymour Hersh did not cause My Lai. He only told the truth about it. Was he a prophet? Why? Why not?

Our study of truth, and the consequences of either avoiding truth or lying, has led us to some very harsh truths:

1. *Being a truth-teller is without a doubt one of the most difficult values people are asked to express.* Perhaps it is because it is so difficult that we find so much lying or evasion of the truth in every society.

2. *Truth-telling can get one into trouble with one's fellows,* but lying and its ally, stealing, can erode the foundation of society.

3. *The value of truth-telling involves every one of us all the time.* It has to do with what we do when we know we won't be caught. The kind of society and the kind of world we end up living in will ultimately depend on what we do about telling the truth. There is no justification for being a liar on the basis of "well, everyone else does it, why shouldn't I?" People can't lie themselves and then complain about the terrible way things are or about how we can't believe or trust "them." We are "them."

IV

Justice

ONE of the tragedies of our time is the absence of great prophetic figures capable of hurling their moral thunderbolts against the evils of this era, eloquent enough to shake ordinary people out of their apathy and self-worship. Who speaks for God's justice? Who indicts the exploiters, the mean-hearted, the narrow-visioned? Who frames the vision of a greathearted and human community, as the Hebrew prophets of old did in their generations? Who makes demands on our conscience, challenges our life-style?

Our politicians seem to pander to the lowest common denominator of public opinion, fingers lifted timidly to the wind. Our religious leaders shrink from controversy because, after all, it could cost membership and antagonize the powerful. The youth rebellion of the sixties petered out to become the stale passivity and complacency of the seventies. Who will speak for justice in the future—and, more to the point, who will listen?

What would happen if, by imagination or fantasy, we could conjure up an unlikely Hebrew prophet in our midst? What would he or she think? What would he or she say? Where would he or she go? And how would we all respond to him or her? Let's see . . .

Marvin was a pickle salesman operating out of a small plant in New England. One day he was flying to New York City to do business with his best account. Suddenly, a violent storm broke out, the plane shuddered crazily, and lightning flashed through the windows. Marvin thought he was doomed. For the first time in a very very long while, Marvin began to pray. "God, O God, help!" Suddenly, in his panic, he thought he heard a voice saying, "Choose life and live."

"I choose, I choose," murmured Marvin desperately.

"Yes, you will live. But you must do my work on earth, for from this moment on you are my servant, Deutero-Isaiah. Put away your pickles, pick up my Torah, and go and prophesy."

The plane landed safely. Dazed, Marvin proceeded to his customer's delicatessen, as planned. "I just came by to thank you for everything and to tell you I'm quitting the pickle business."

"Why?" asked the boss at the deli. "You getting too proud to sell pickles, Marv, old boy?"

"No," replied Marvin. "You see, I'm no longer Marvin. From this moment forth, my name is Deutero-Isaiah. I have been told to quit pickles because the world is in an even bigger pickle, and to go forth and prophesy to my people, that they may be saved."

The boss smirked. "Yeah? Who said?"

"God. It was the voice of God."

"God?" repeated the boss, bemused. "I thought I told you not to talk to strangers in this town." He roared at his own joke. "Okay, Marvin—I mean Deutero—if that's what you want, I wish you luck. You'll need it."

Deutero went into a shop and got some prophet's garb —an old robe, a loin cloth, gray sneakers, and a sweat band for his flowing hair. He then took off to stroll about the city, seeing everything with fresh eyes, as if for the first time. Imbued with a hunger for justice, a divine fire in his belly, he watched old men and women sitting on the benches along Broadway—alone, blank-eyed, and terrified of young people—and he visited a nursing home for elderly people, which looked more like a warehouse for those not yet lucky enough to die. And he cried out:

They are abandoned like old clothes, for it is a throw-away
society/
It obsolesces people/
Of what benefit their labor?/
A generation cometh, a generation goeth/
And the young are celebrated and old age is a stigma.

Who nourishes their dignity/
Does no one share with them so that/
they will know "to be old is a wonderful thing when one
has not unlearned what it means to begin."

Buber

New York City is a big town, so Deutero hired a guide and
a car to take him about. In the latter part of the twentieth
century, how far can a prophet go on foot? Maybe Hillel
could teach on one foot, but not Deutero. The guide es-
corted him around the city, showing him the grandeur of
Fifth Avenue, Wall Street, Park Avenue, the museums, the
United Nations, as well as the devastation of the South Bronx
and the dismal slums of Harlem and sections of Brooklyn.
Deutero seemed fascinated, soaking in every experience,
asking questions, measuring everything against some inter-
nal and eternal yardstick, alternately exalted and incensed
by what he saw.

The guide drove him to the United Nations and
Deutero, impressed because he had never before been inside the sleek structure, tried to enter the General Assembly
to join the debate.

A uniformed guard, looking him over disdainfully, demanded his ticket.

"No, no, no," protested Deutero, trying to brush him
aside. "I was told to come here. I'm to speak to the world."

"Which delegation invited you?" the guard demanded.

"Not a delegation, sir. God!"

"Oh, boy, another loon out of the cracker barrel!!" he
shouted, calling a fellow guard to help push the prophet out
onto the street.

Thoughtfully, the guide led the prophet across the street to the outside courtyard and the Isaiah Wall, pointing to the prophetic legend containing Isaiah's words: "And they shall beat their swords into plowshares and their spears into pruning hooks, And nation shall not lift up sword against nation, neither shall they make war anymore."

Deutero stood and stared, and then, to the consternation of the guide, he began to shout:

Peace, peace, but there is no peace.
The nations give lip service to God's demand that they pursue peace.
But they exhaust their resources on machines of destruction.
They prate of peace in these glass echo chambers, but they build missiles which can destroy the world and kill each of my children ten times over.

A billion human beings go to bed hungry every night while half of humankind diets.
They place their reliance not on God, but on nuclear bombs and poisonous missiles, on might and power.
And humanity lives on the knife-edge of holocaust.
Is this the path I have directed?
To live in fear and trembling, like a small animal entrapped in the jungle;
To turn science into mad schemes against human life;
To contemplate the mass suicide of the human race—
Jonestown writ large—and to call this national security;
To risk the obliteration of God's earth?
No, *this* is the path I have mandated:
To seek peace and pursue it.
To tend the widow, the elderly, the hungry, and the weak.
To nurture the tendrils of life.
To open the blind eye and to lift the heavy burden of fear and poverty.
And to make the right to go forth upon the earth.

By this time, Deutero's voice had gathered force and it resonated through the area. A small crowd gathered around, mildly interested. They had listened to a hundred other demonstrators. This one was dressed a bit more shabbily, and his voice was unusually loud, but that was about it. He made no more sense than the other agitators.

A bored police officer wandered up, asked if Deutero had a permit to demonstrate, and then said, "Okay, buster, let's move it." The guide decided it was a good time to push the prophet into the car and move on.

Driving through Brooklyn, Deutero demanded that the car be stopped. He raced into the nearest building—a crumbling, filthy tenement—and gazed at the gaping holes in the wall, the littered stairwell, the broken plaster, the smashed windows, the sullen faces. Softly, he tried to speak to the tenants.

Most of them ignored him; some called him "honkie"; one thought he was another derelict or pusher sleeping in the hallway and tried to chase him away. A few finally spoke to him, answering his questions, explaining how they came to live in such a hovel, what it was like for them to try to raise their children amid rats and rotting garbage and uncaring welfare workers and bitter landlords, and trying to explain the hatred festering among whites, blacks, Hispanics, and Asians. Deutero sat down on the front stoop and sobbed. His eyes reflected terror. He trembled. He tried to speak several times and his voice was husky and muffled. At last, he spoke, his voice an uncertain trumpet:

> Listen, you who are deaf;
> You blind ones, look up and see!
>
> Yet it is a people plundered and despoiled:
> All of them are trapped in holes,
> Imprisoned in dungeons.
> They are given over to plunder, with none to rescue them;
> To despoilment, with none to say "Give back!"
>
> Isa. 42:18, 22

The guide was feeling guilty because Deutero was so upset. His trip so far was really depressing. He determined to brighten Deutero's day, to show him beauty, to cheer him up. So they visited the magnificent Cloisters, an adjunct of the Metropolitan Museum of Art, on the heights overlooking the Hudson River. Later they drove to a marina where Deutero stood on the bank of the glistening river. Looking out to the New Jersey Palisades from the Manhattan side, the Hudson was sparkling and wondrous like a picture postcard. Deutero looked down and placed his hand in the water. When he withdrew it, it was dark and slimy from pollution.

"How dare they!" Deutero shouted, his face flushed.

"Look, don't get excited," said the guide. "We're slowly cleaning up the river. It's already much better than it was. And, you know, there's lots of needed industry along the river, and you can't really stop progress."

Deutero stared at the guide balefully and then looked back at the despoiled river. He spoke:

> Woe to the person who stands on the earth and does not see what he sees, for in every drop of water in the sea and in every grain of dust in the earth have I created its own image.

Getting a little panicky, the guide decided to get the prophet out of the city, with all its intractable urban problems, and into the country and the loveliness of a quiet, tree-lined suburb. And Deutero did seem to relax; he actually dozed off during a traffic jam on the Long Island Expressway. Getting out of the car in a pleasant suburb, Deutero nodded and smiled at passersby. That was a mistake. A police car suddenly appeared, and an officer walked toward him and said: "You live around here? The people around here are uptight about strangers. Lots of robberies and even some muggings. What business do you have in this neighborhood?" The guide, embarrassed for Deutero, muttered something about civil rights and the A.C.L.U., and the policeman said, "Watch it. This is a nice neighborhood. No trouble! Mind your own business!"

"Is it a crime to walk around this neighborhood? Is this a prison?" Deutero asked the guide. "Where are all the people who live in these homes? Why are the streets empty?"

"Watching television, mostly," he replied. "They stay home a lot—scared, you see. The neighborhood is beginning to change, you know what I mean?"

Deutero responded:

> They are enjoined to welcome the stranger and to love their neighbors as themselves.
> But they do not even know their neighbors.
> They live in boxes classified by class and color and status.
> They know who does *not* belong in their neighborhood.
> And they are connected not to each other—to neighbors, to community, to family—but umbilically to a television set and to an automobile.
>
> They do not have time to read, to talk, to form community.
> For life is a fever of work and commuting and flying and drinking and playing and hypertension and self-gratification.
> What remains of the human person? Where is human dignity? What is man and woman that God should care about them? What is the purpose of it all?
> I made them a little lower than angels and they have made themselves pleasure machines and collectors of things.
> I blew into them the fire of soul, spirit, inner life—the deepest qualities of humanity.
> And they have separated themselves from Me, each other, and even themselves.

"Come off it," cried the guide. "You say you're a prophet, okay, anything goes in this crazy town, but you are really an awful *kvetch*, nothing satisfies you. These are basically good people. They work hard, they are honest, they are God-fearing, they belong to fine synagogues and churches, and they give to Israel, Community Chest, and the Red Cross. Be fair, after all, I mean."

Deutero exclaimed:

> I made a covenant with them alone.
> I entrusted them with a mission.
> Not merely to be nice and honest and not to beat up strangers or steal from the blind.
> I enjoined them to be something new under the sun—a holy people, a kingdom of priests, copartners with God in completing the work of creation.

"Tell me, guide, has that bargain been kept?"

"Come with me. I'll show you, Deutero. I'll take you to the synagogue. It's beautiful. You'll love it."

And so they went to a temple. It was, of course, not to be compared with the Temple of Jerusalem, but it was gracious, and lovely, and modern indeed. Deutero seemed to enjoy the architecture and the style, and especially the words inscribed above the ark in the sanctuary: "Know before whom you stand."

Deutero stood in the hallway and listened to what the guide described as a "meeting of the temple board." The voices carried easily to the hallway because there were lively and sometimes angry exchanges. The voices rose and fell, arguing about the deficit, the cantor's contract, what to charge for use of the building for bar and bat mitvah parties, what to do about a small group of dissidents who intended to challenge the Administration slate, how to increase membership, how to welcome new members, how to get the organ fixed, whether to have an appeal for funds on Yom Kippur.

"This is a temple?" asked Deutero in bafflement. "It is more like a marketplace. Like the front office of the pickle factory. They have no time for God."

"No. You don't understand. It's not that. It's just that this is not the Sabbath or a holy day. This is not a service. The board is doing the practical business of the synagogue."

Deutero pushed open the door and thundered to the startled board of trustees: Practical? Business?

> Where were you when I laid the foundations of the earth?
> Tell me if you have understanding.
> Who determined its measurements—surely you know!
> Or who stretched the line upon it?
> Have you commanded the morning since your days began,
> And caused the dawn to know its place?
> Have you entered into the springs of the sea
> Or walked in the recesses of the deep?
> Have you comprehended the expanse of the earth?
> Declare, if you know all this.
>
> Job 38:4–5, 12, 16, 18

The president interrupted Deutero and placed a threatening hand on his elbow. "This is a private building, sir. We're having an important meeting. You have no business here. What are you jabbering about anyway? Just leave quietly or we'll have to call the police. Look at you, you have some nerve coming in here dressed like that. No tie. A mess. What are you, a crazy jogger or something? Where the hell is the custodian anyway? How can they let a nut like this wander around here like it's Grand Central Station?"

Deutero paled. "This is Judaism? This is the Lord's holy temple? This is the work of His hands?"

A young person rose and placed an arm gently on Deutero's shoulder and led him out of the room. "I'm the rabbi. Please excuse my president. He gets excited. Look, you fellows come around here once a month or so, and I'm always glad to help. You should have come to my office, not barged into the board meeting. Anyway, I have a little discretionary fund, enough for a good meal and to get you transportation out of town."

"Thank you," said Deutero. "But I'm not a beggar, I'm a prophet."

"Of course," smiled the rabbi warmly. "Aren't we all?

New York is a good place to visit, but a terror to be a prophet in. But if it isn't money, call me tomorrow to make an appointment and we'll talk, okay?"

"Talk?" murmured Deutero. "About what would we talk?"

"Look, you're under stress. I know the symptoms. Happens to all of us. We live in a pressure cooker, right? One too many hassles and we explode, right? So you call tomorrow, okay, and we'll get you some help."

"God sent me," Deutero said. "He called me from the pickle factory."

"Oy," sighed the rabbi. "For God's sake, what *do* you want, anyway?"

The prophet said, "He has told you, O man, what is good and what the Lord requires of you: Only to do justice and to love goodness, and to walk modestly with your God" (Mic. 6:8).

Our scenario is a bit melodramatic, but it is no doubt true that a prophet would meet frustration, repression, and ridicule by trying to plumb-line God's justice against the issues of our time. In our fantasy script, Deutero cries out against nuclear armaments, our treatment of the elderly, slums, pollution, bigotry, and religious hypocrisy. But in truth, for most of the urgent issues of our time, it is no longer simple —even for a prophet—to decide what is right and what is wrong. It is not difficult to decry ghettos, but what solution would be just? It is easy to condemn a nuclear arms race, but what is the alternative? Is it pacifism and disarmament? Then who would restrain the lawless and aggressive nations? Would pacifism have been a just response to Hitlerism? Similarly, it is easy, and fashionable, to condemn pollution—but can the energy crisis be overcome without trading off some environmental controls? And what about the need for jobs to get those poor people out of the slums? Can enough jobs be created if environmental justice is our only concern?

Justice in our time is more complex. What once seemed a simple choice of good or bad now seems to be a dilemma, a conflict of two goods, or two bads, or a shade of gray. Racial segregation is bad; but is a benign quota, such as a maximum 30 percent minority in a community's housing, right or wrong?

What is justice? Fair dealing among people. Why should we strive to be just? According to prophetic Judaism, because God has enjoined us to do so. Is justice only concerned with our face-to-face personal encounters? No. Justice also compels our involvement in the broader issues of social justice. Justice for the mentally ill, for example. Justice for the handicapped. Justice for ethnic groups about whom some still make jokes. Justice for the neglected veterans of Vietnam. Justice for those locked into prison.

Why is justice so crucial? Because it is what keeps us human. Without justice, human beings consume each other like cannibals. What does God really want of us? As Deutero told us, the prophet Micah said it best: "Only to do justice and to love goodness, and to walk modestly with your God." It is no accident that justice came first.

Justice, in the words of Micah, is clearly defined. It is *doing*. It is *loving*. It is *walking modestly*. All are action words. All demand something of the doer. No person can be just who loves people in the abstract but hates the individuals met in the real world. No person can be just who wants to see justice done but personally acts in ways that are dishonest or unfair.

The prophets were the first to link God with our relationships to others. Just as the Jewish religion was the first to bring the world the idea of one God, so did that one God demand that we serve God by dealing justly with one another.

Nothing angered the prophets more than seeing their people keeping the form of Judaism while ignoring the poor, or neglecting strangers or cheating customers at the merchants' scales. There has rarely been a more blistering attack

on this kind of hypocrisy than the one Isaiah leveled at his
people in God's name:

> Bringing oblations is futile,
> Incense is offensive to Me.
> New moon and sabbath,
> Proclaiming of solemnities,
> Assemblies with iniquity,
> I cannot abide.
> Your new moons and fixed seasons
> Fill Me with loathing;
> They are become a burden to Me,
> I cannot endure them.
> And when you lift up your hands,
> I will turn My eyes away from you;
> Though you pray at length,
> I will not listen.
> Your hands are stained with crime.

Isa. 1:13–15

God does not want us only to *believe*. We must also follow
God's *ways* and *commandments*. And if we refuse? Then
the fabric of trust begins to unravel. Society begins to come
apart at the seams. Violence, hatred, and war are the bitter
fruits of injustice. So justice is not merely a good, or even
godly, idea. It is the only sure guarantee of a human society
in which people can live their lives as human beings, with
trust in each other, with trust in society, and with confidence
in the future.

There is something radical about the teachings of the
prophets, even for our own time. Most religions teach that
a person can be saved only by believing the right things.
Judaism has always had a different point of view. To the
prophets, what you believe (or say you believe) is not as
important as what you do! Belief is less important than right
conduct. In fact, the proof of the pudding of belief is in the
eating—in action, in *life*. Judaism recognized that one
becomes what one does. Once God was quoted as saying
about the Jewish people: "Would that they forgot about Me

and remembered My Commandments." What do you think was meant by that? It means that Judaism is a way of life.

Prophetic Judaism has always cared less about saving the soul of an individual than about saving the whole society by bringing God's justice and mercy to all its inhabitants. How can you really save a person if the whole society goes rotten? Or, if the world is polluted or destroyed by nuclear war? This emphasis on social justice, on changing the world for the better, is one of the reasons so many Jews in our time have worked for civil rights, laws to help the poor and the weak, and disarmament and peace among nations. Justice is a Jewish addiction, our social disease; the prophets were hooked on it; they made the pursuit of justice a central task for the Jew in every generation. Part of our mission, our purpose on the earth, is to share with God in perfecting the world for all humankind.

INDIVIDUAL VERSUS SOCIAL JUSTICE

There are two major categories of justice, *individual* and *social*. *Individual* justice is treating each person around you with kindness and fairness. Do you think this is harder to do with those closest to you—your brothers, sisters, parents, cousins—than with those farther away—classmates, neighborhood pals, teachers? The biblical writers told us to "love your neighbor as yourself." Is that possible? Certainly it is not easy, especially if we don't love, or value, ourselves enough. Those who don't respect themselves will have a rough time respecting others. Most criminals, for example, are people who have a very poor self-image.

Social justice, on the other hand, is taking some responsibility for the larger problems of the community. For example, the American Indians have been mistreated since the moment white people drove them out by colonizing America. They are mistreated still. Social justice requires taking some responsibility to do something to right the wrongs that all Americans have done to the original settlers of this land, even if you personally never meet or come in contact with any individual native American. This means reading up on the problem, knowing the facts, maybe raising money for an organization for Indian rights; perhaps writing to your congressional representatives and senators asking that they take action. Perhaps it might mean visiting an Indian reservation while vacationing with your family or, when you are older, working as an Action volunteer in an Indian community.

But you cannot morally say, "This is not *my* problem," or "I don't know anything about it." These are the excuses most "good" Germans made while our fellow Jews were being slaughtered by the Nazis. What Judaism demands is "Do not profit by the blood of your brother or sister . . ." And your brother or sister is poor, old, black, Puerto Rican, Indian, white, and Vietnamese, as well as Jewish! Saying something is not your problem is like drilling a hole in your end of a boat. It may be "your" end of the boat but a hole so drilled will sink the entire craft. Lack of empathy for another's pain is the gaping hole in the human boat. In our tradition, saving one person is the equivalent of saving the world.

Sometimes it is easy to know what is just and what is unjust. In the case of the Indians, a clear-cut injustice has been done—and it is *just* to work for an end to the poverty, misery, and ill health in which Indians in America still live. But how? Is it better to integrate Indians into the mainstream of American life, or to preserve Indian culture on their own reservations? Which do Indians want? Can integration and ethnic identity be reconciled? Which solutions are right?

Clearly, some issues of justice are not cut-and-dried. Sometimes there simply is not good on one side and bad on the other, but good and bad on each side, and it is necessary to choose the greater good or the lesser evil. Sometimes by *not* acting one can contribute to injustice. Let us say that two candidates are running for the president of the class.

You don't think either one is super, so you don't bother to vote. Wouldn't it have been better, though harder, to examine which of the two was more qualified, or at least less harmful, and to take the trouble to choose? Some of the worst politicians in America won public office because too many voters said both candidates were poor, and so didn't bother to vote. Some 60 percent of the American people don't bother to vote for President of the United States.

Just as it is usually easier to do nothing, sometimes it seems more rewarding to be unjust. A storekeeper, for example, mistakenly gives you a ten instead of a one dollar bill in change. So why be good, just, moral? One reason, of course, is the fear of getting caught and punished. Another is the need to be trusted and to trust others. Another is conscience, which is the police officer of trust. This is what nags at us when we do wrong. It makes us slightly ashamed of ourselves. Where does conscience come from? Does everyone have it?

Some believe that conscience is the stirrings of God acting inside our own being. How do you feel about that? What does this mean? Rabbi Barnett Brickner once defined God as the "highest you can think, the deepest you can feel, and the best you can do." If this is God, perhaps you can understand why some people see God as conscience stirring inside of us—particularly when you ignore your finest impulses.

Since Judaism believes that justice gives life meaning and purpose, that life is exalted through righteousness, it demands that parents teach the values of justice to their children. According to the Bible, God said of Abraham, the first Jew: "For I have singled him out, that he may instruct his children and his posterity to keep the way of the Lord by doing what is just and right, in order that the Lord may bring about for Abraham what He has promised him " (Gen 18:19). The Lord said: "I will make of you a great nation, and I will bless you; I will make your name great, and you shall be a blessing: I will bless those who bless you, and curse him that curses you; all the families of the earth shall bless themselves by you" (Gen. 12:2,3).

But, you can say, if God wants justice and is all-powerful, how can God permit so much injustice? How can God permit the butchery in wars, the persecution of so many peoples, the misery of millions, the pollution of the planet? The Jewish answer is that human beings are not puppets. We are free to do good or bad. We have choices. We are responsible for human destiny. God does not start wars; human beings do. God does not poison the air and the water; we do. God does not make color a badge of shame; we do. God is a standard, a goal, an ideal for human endeavor. If we reject the standard and fall short of the goal, that can't be blamed on God. We can't pass the buck to God for our shortcomings. Justice to others is one of the things that God demands of us, and that each of us expects from the other because our fates are interwoven.

How do you think Jews in your town are carrying out their mission as champions of justice? Is there a social action committee in your temple? Is there a Jewish Community Relations Council in town? What do they do? Find out. Does your youth group work on community problems to bring justice to the less privileged? How?

What can you and other people in your class do to promote justice in your town? Invite young people from church groups to join you in a project. Start a mitzvah corps project? Raise money for needy Jews in the community? Circulate petitions for human rights, in behalf of Soviet Jews, or to end pollution? Visit the elderly? Organize a message center at the temple to work for good laws? Adopt a Vietnamese family? What else? The mission of the young is the hope for the future. The prophet Joel taught us that "Your old men shall dream dreams, and your young men shall see visions" (Joel 3:1). A just society is the shining vision of the Hebrew prophets. Our never-ending Jewish mission is to make it happen. Jewish young people inherit this legacy of glory and grandeur. It is no small gift.

V

Chosen People

Six million Jews were killed in the Holocaust. Hitler's
goal to make Central and Eastern Europe totally *Judenrein,*
emptied of its Jewish population, was nearly realized.

A few years ago a Jewish thinker, Dr. Emil Fackenheim,
writing about the implications of that genocide, expressed
the thought that Jews must not allow Hitler "a posthumous
victory." In other words, since Hitler came so close to elimi-
nating the Jews of the world, we Jews who survive must not,
by our rejection of our Jewish identity, give Hitler the goal
he sought to reach, a world free of Jews. It is a compelling
thought, and many Jews today feel that Dr. Fackenheim is
correct. Elie Wiesel, the author, put it this way:

> Jews are forbidden to hand Hitler posthumous victories.
> They are commanded to survive as Jews, lest the Jewish
> people perish. They are commanded to remember the vic-
> tims of Auschwitz, lest their memory perish. They are for-
> bidden to despair of man and his world and to escape into
> either cynicism or otherworldliness, lest they cooperate in
> delivering the world over to the forces of Auschwitz. Fi-
> nally, they are forbidden to despair of the God of Israel, lest
> Judaism perish. A secularist Jew cannot make himself be-
> lieve by a mere act of will, nor can he be commanded to
> do so . . . And a religious Jew who has stayed with his God
> may be forced into new, possibly revolutionary relation-
> ships with Him. One possibility, however, is wholly un-
> thinkable. A Jew may not respond to Hitler's attempt to
> destroy Judaism by himself cooperating in its destruction.

In ancient times, the unthinkable Jewish sin was idolatry.
Today it is to respond to Hitler by doing his work.

How can or should we, the surviving Jewish community of
the world, retain and preserve our Jewish identity and insure the future for our offspring? By isolating ourselves from
the rest of society? By living in Jewish ghettos, hoping that
the corrosive influences of the outside world do not erode
that identity? Some Jews have taken that approach. By
creating a separate Jewish nation? Obviously, the existence
of the State of Israel is an expression of that approach. By
preserving the culture and the traditions of the group that
give it its distinct character? That, too, is a real option
through which to keep the group intact. What about developing and clinging to an idea to give the group a sense of
cohesiveness? It is done all the time. Think of the slogans
"God Bless America," "Black is Beautiful," "Proud and Pol-
ish"—or, in our case, "We Jews are the Chosen People."

Chosen People, indeed! Does that idea make you a little
uncomfortable? If so, why?

If it does, it indicates how real and how powerful an idea
can be.

We usually think of reality in terms of our senses—
sight, sound, touch, smell. A tree is real. Tears are real; so
is laughter. But ideas are also real. Ideas can cause you to
do or not do something. They can affect your physical
body. Psychiatrists will tell you that a person can lose the
use of a limb because of an idea in the head which para-
lyzes the limb. Psychosomatic illnesses and phobias are
very real illnesses, caused by what a person may be thinking and feeling—caused by ideas. Clearly, reality does not
have to do only with what we call the physical senses. Reality can be as much in a person's head—invisible—as it can
be anywhere. Ideas are the most REAL of all matters.
Ideas have the power to change the world. And they have
done so often.

Strange as it may seem, the idea that Jews are the Chosen People has kept millions of Jews alive and caused the death of millions more; it has inspired people willingly to give up their lives and at various times in history it has elevated, angered, and embarrassed more people than almost any other idea in the history of the western world.

Some idea! How did we get it, and why are we stuck with it? More important, is it worth preserving in this post-Holocaust age where we dare not give Hitler a posthumous victory?

THE IDEA OF THE JEWS AS A CHOSEN PEOPLE: HOW IT BEGAN

A midrash quotes God as saying to our ancestors: "Had it not been for your acceptance of My Torah, I would not have given you any special recognition, nor would I have treated you any better than idolators" (Exodus Rabbah 47:3).

The implication is clear: The choice was mutual. God chose the Jews to be God's people on the condition that the Jewish people would accept upon themselves the yoke of the Torah, the responsibility for fulfilling God's commandments to be just and ethical in their behavior.

According to the biblical story, when Abraham was ninety-nine years old, the Lord appeared to him and said: "Walk in My ways and be blameless. I will establish My covenant between Me and you" (Gen. 17:1–2).

Notice that the phrase "walk in My ways and be blameless" comes before "I will establish My covenant." Only if the Jewish people kept their part of the bargain was God obliged to fulfill God's part. And what were the people's obligations? The Book of Deuteronomy makes it clear: "The Lord will establish you as His holy people, as He swore to you, if you keep the commandments of the Lord your God and walk in His ways " (Deut. 28:9). The same "if-then" conditions are stated in Exodus:

> Now then, if you will obey Me faithfully and keep My
> covenant, you shall be My treasured possession among all
> the peoples. Indeed, all the earth is Mine, but you shall be
> to Me a kingdom of priests and a holy nation.
>
> Exod. 19:5–6

As the blessings for fulfilling their end of the contract (or
berit, Hebrew for "covenant") are spelled out, so too are the
penalties if they fail to keep their part of the berit:

> But if you do not heed the word of the Lord your God to
> observe faithfully all His commandments and laws which
> I enjoin upon you this day, all these curses shall come upon
> you and take effect: Cursed shall you be in the city and
> cursed shall you be in the country.
>
> Deut. 28:15–16

> (The rest of chapter 28 details many more penalties for not
> fulfilling the berit.)

But why did God choose the Jews? Why not other nations,
stronger and more numerous than the Israelites? Again, the
biblical text gives us a clue. Moses says to the people:

> It is not because you are the most numerous of peoples that
> the Lord set His heart on you and chose you—indeed, you
> are the smallest of peoples; but it was because the Lord
> loved you and kept the oath He made to your fathers that
> the Lord freed you with a mighty hand and rescued you
> from the house of bondage, from the power of Pharaoh
> king of Egypt.
>
> Deut. 7:7–8

This promise by God to the earliest Hebrews, to be their
God and to protect them, was repeated over and over again
in the earliest biblical narratives. Each of the patriarchs
renewed the commitment to the berit. Isaac recognized
God's protective presence (Gen. 26:3–6), and Jacob was
bound in covenant with the Mighty One (Gen. 28:10–22).

Did God actually choose the Jewish people to the exclu-
sion of all others? No one really knows. On the surface, it
seems unlikely. But what is important is that the people of
Israel *thought* God had chosen them, and they acted on that
idea. And that made all the difference!

The people began to believe that they were God's people, that God had chosen them and was Israel's God. Moreover, they believed that God had chosen the Hebrew people
from all the peoples of the earth to exemplify God's law,
God's justice, God's mercy, God's greatness to the entire
world. They were to be a model for the world, a light unto
the nations. As we shall see, the prophets of Israel later
developed this theme fully. In so doing, they saved the people of Israel; they gave them hope, a sense of purpose and
national pride when stronger nations ground their faces into
the dust of captivity. It gave them a reason to continue
following the commandments of their Lord at a time when
such observance seemed otherwise absurd.

Considering oneself a *chosen* person can be pretty
heady stuff. It can make one smug and self-centered. It is
easy to develop the idea that, as a Chosen People, a group
can do no wrong. People can begin to feel that they are
above reproach, for after all, God is on their side. That is
exactly what began to happen to the people of Israel, particularly during the eighth century B.C.E.

The reign of King Jeroboam II in northern Israel was a
time of great prosperity. It was also a time of pervasive
moral corruption in Israel. The people were convinced that
they could do no wrong and that "the day of the Lord," for
which they constantly prayed, would be a time of supreme
national glory. They believed that the covenant meant that,
so long as they brought their sacrifices and offered their
ceremonial observances, they would be safe and secure. But
they were living with a false sense of security.

THE DEMAND OF AMOS

The prophet Amos told them in scathing terms how wrong they were. Chosenness, he said, did not mean privilege. On the contrary, it meant added responsibility and extra penalties for breaking the moral demands of the covenant. Precisely because God entered into a berit with *you,* said Amos, you are particularly responsible.

> You alone have I singled out
> Of all the families of the earth—
> That is why I will call you to account
> For all your iniquities.
>
> Amos 3:2

The great Day of the Lord, for which they so eagerly prayed, would come, but not as a day of light and rejoicing.

> Ah, you who wish
> For the day of the Lord!
> Why should you want
> The day of the Lord?
> It shall be darkness, not light!
> —As if a man should run from a lion
> And be attacked by a bear;
> Or if he got indoors,
> Should lean his hand on the wall
> And be bitten by a snake!
> Surely the day of the Lord shall be
> Not light, but darkness,
> Blackest night without a glimmer.
>
> Amos 5:18–20

Being chosen will not spare you from God's wrath, he continued. You have failed to "let justice well up like waters, [and] righteousness like an unfailing stream" (Amos 5:24), and you will pay for the error of your ways.

So critical was Amos of the people's drift away from the

purpose of election that in one passage he seemed even to deny the very idea of chosenness:

> To Me, O Israelites, you are
> Just like the Ethiopians
>
> —declares the Lord.
>
> True, I brought Israel up
> From the land of Egypt,
> But also the Philistines from Caphtor
> And the Arameans from Kir.
>
> Amos 9:7

We refer to this passage elsewhere to exemplify the concept of God's universality. It is precisely that universality the prophet had in mind when he rejected the people's false idea that their God was only a national god, to be mobilized to serve Israel's exclusive interests. If the people thought that the idea of election or chosenness meant that God served Israel, rather than the other way around, they were wrong. God is active in the histories of other nations, too, even as God is active in Israelite history. But with Israel, God demands more. When they entered into the covenant, Israel knew what God demanded. Therefore, because the people could not plead ignorance of the ethical demands placed upon them, they had to be judged more severely than any other nation. By those standards, they failed. Amos prophesied their destruction.

But, doesn't the concept of chosenness allow for error and repentance? Is there no mercy to be shown to those who seek to change their ways? The ethical demands of the berit are so severe that no nation can constantly live up to all of them. Where is the compassion, the love? Shouldn't God be merciful?

THE MERCY OF HOSEA

These questions and this plea were not without merit. One prophet tried to respond. His name was Hosea. He prophesied at the same time as Amos, about 735 B.C.E. His entire life reflected the message that God's love could soften the severe justice demanded by Amos.

Hosea was the first Israelite prophet to interpret the covenant by comparing it with a marriage. Hosea used the image of a sacred marriage between God and Israel to illustrate his philosophy. The symbol of this marriage came to him from his own marriage to Gomer, a prostitute. Yes, prostitution existed even in ancient Israel. In those days, sex was glorified by nature religions. People engaged in acts of sacred prostitution in order to increase the fertility of field and flock. Daringly, Hosea had bought Gomer off an auction block, taken her to his home, and loved her as his wife. Soon, however, home life became too confining for Gomer. She left, and reverted to her former profession. According to Hosea, that was exactly what Israel did. The "wife" whom God has chosen had become a whore, selling her soul to idolatrous gods. Israel lacked *chesed*, steadfast love, that loyalty that binds two parties to one another.

The entire prophetic Book of Hosea is built on the parallel between the love of a man and a woman and the love of God for the people of Israel.

Hosea loved Gomer and took her back. So, too, did God love Israel and would take her back if only she would leave her idolatrous ways. God would not abandon this people.

> How can I give you up, O Ephraim?
> How surrender you, O Israel?
> How can I make you like Admah,
> Render you like Zeboiim?
> I have had a change of heart,
> All My tenderness is stirred.
> I will not act on My wrath,
> Will not turn to destroy Ephraim.

For I am God, not man,
The Holy One in your midst:
I will not come in fury.

Hos. 11:8–9

The deepest note struck in the Book of Hosea is the proclamation that God's anger is not designed to punish the people, but to redeem them. God's purpose is not to destroy, but to heal.

Return, O Israel, to the Lord your God,
For you have fallen because of your sin.

Hos. 14:2

Parents also become angry with their children. When they punish them, it is not usually because they no longer love them but, on the contrary, because they love them so much that they want to help them do better. Children sometimes have trouble understanding that kind of love, particularly when they are angry as a result of punishment.

The people failed to heed the prophet's plea. Disaster followed. In 721 B.C.E., Sargon II, king of Assyria, overran northern Israel and took the people captive. They are known as the Ten Lost Tribes of Israel, because they became lost forever in the mists of history. Only the southern tribes of Judah remained. Their spiritual center was the Temple in Jerusalem. The century that followed was a dark and difficult time for the remnant of the once mighty Hebrew people.

JEREMIAH—THE NEW COVENANT

The great prophetic figure who dominated this period was Jeremiah (626–586 B.C.E.). He began to prophesy "in the thirteenth year of [Josiah's] reign," about 626 B.C.E. His early prophecies borrowed heavily from those of his predecessor,

Hosea. Israel again was portrayed as a bride who became unfaithful to her husband. But God is ready to forgive and take back the people if only they will repent (see Jer. 2:1–3 and chapters 3–4).

This prophetic call for a reformation of the spirit fit perfectly with King Josiah's own desires. This period, marked by the breakup of the old Assyrian empire and the emergence of Babylonia, was the perfect time to initiate such a process of national renewal.

Josiah's Reform

In the year 621 B.C.E., at a time when the Temple was being repaired, a scroll of the Torah was discovered within the Temple precincts (see 2 Kings 22:3–10 for the biblical account). The contents were read to the king. They warned that evil would come upon the city because the people had not lived up to God's ethical demands. Josiah took advantage of this discovery to begin a great royal reform. He immediately summoned the people to the Temple for a ceremony of covenant renewal, where he read "the scroll of the covenant" to them. On the basis of this scroll, the people reaffirmed their covenant, to follow God and to obey the commandments. Josiah's declaration of independence from Assyria could hardly have been made in clearer terms. All "high places" (other altars, usually on hilltops) were eliminated, and worship was concentrated in the Temple in Jerusalem.

At first, Jeremiah supported the new reform. But soon he became discouraged. He seemed to sense that something was missing. Obedience or disobedience could not be measured by a code of rules set down in a book. People could not win God's blessing only by devoting themselves to an external code of rules. The will to be decent had to come from the heart.

And so, toward the end of his life, Jeremiah began to preach a remarkably new idea. There would be a fresh beginning for the people of Israel:

See, a time is coming—declares the Lord—when I will make a new covenant with the House of Israel and the House of Judah. It will not be like the covenant I made with their fathers, when I took them by the hand to lead them out of the land of Egypt, a covenant which they broke, so that I rejected them—declares the Lord. But such is the covenant I will make with the House of Israel after these days—declares the Lord: I will put My Teaching into their inmost being and inscribe it upon their hearts. Then I will be their God, and they shall be My people. No longer will they need to teach one another and say to one another, "Heed the Lord"; for all of them, from the least of them to the greatest, shall heed Me—declares the Lord.

For I will forgive their iniquities,
And remember their sins no more.

Jer. 31:31–34

This was undoubtedly one of the most important treatments of the idea of covenant that Judaism had ever seen. Notice that the prophet implied the end of the "if-then" relationship between God and the people. No longer would the fulfillment of the covenant be dependent on obeying written laws or a code put together by legal experts. In the period of *the new covenant,* Jews would know God's demands, since the Teaching would be "inscribed" on their hearts. This was, of course, a poetic way of saying that people would internalize those ethical demands associated with the berit, and would do them automatically. Such a time would give birth to a new relationship between God and the people, a time when no one would have to be instructed in ethical behavior. Such a time would truly be a new age for humankind. Jeremiah's new covenant proclaimed a fervent message of hope, but it could not spare the people from the pain of defeat and exile.

In 597, Babylonia began its conquest of Judah. By 586, the dismantling was complete: the bulk of the Hebrew people were taken into Babylonian exile. There they began to ask themselves: How did this calamity happen to us? Have we not lived up to our end of the covenant? Now how shall we live?

The figure who addressed himself to these troubling questions was the enigmatic prophet of the exile. His name was Ezekiel.

EZEKIEL

You were punished with exile, he told them, because you violated your obligation to the covenant. The exile is not a sign of God's weakness; it is your punishment for falling so far away from what you should have known God wanted. However, the exile will come to an end. God will not permanently abandon you (see Ezek. 36:24–28). The time will come when you will return to your land, where the new covenant about which Jeremiah spoke will be renewed with you (Ezek. 16:60–62). In the meantime, try to understand that God is not bound to the Temple in Jerusalem. You may find God wherever you seek, through meditation, through prayer, through study, even here in the exile. Keep the covenant community, even in the bleakness of exile. And they did.

DEUTERO-ISAIAH: CHOSEN FOR A PURPOSE

At the moment of the people's greatest tragedy, Jeremiah gave them reason to hope. Ezekiel answered their question: How shall we live now that we are exiled? But it was a prophet whose name we do not even know, but who lived during the exile, who gave them a reason for believing they they had a future. You shall survive, this prophet told them, because God has chosen you for a task—a job, a mission. You shall be "a light unto the nations." The prophet who originated such a remarkable idea put down these thoughts in a block of 16 chapters that are found in the book of Isaiah.

They are numbered chapters 40–55, but they are not the work of the first Isaiah. The author of these chapters lived two and a half centuries after the first Isaiah of Israel, under a totally different political situation. We know very little about this prophet, not even a name. We call the prophet Deutero-(or Second) Isaiah, only because these writings were found attached to and included in the Isaiah scroll.

In poetic and moving words, the prophet reminds Israel of the unbroken relationship that continues to exist between God and the people, despite the long void of the exile:

> But you, Israel, My servant,
> Jacob, whom I have chosen,
> Seed of Abraham My friend—
> You whom I drew from the ends of the earth
> And called from its far corners,
> To whom I said: You are My servant;
> I chose you, I have not rejected you.—
> Fear not, for I am with you,
> Be not frightened, for I am your God;
> I strengthen you and I help you,
> I uphold you with My victorious right hand.

Isa. 41:8–10

The message of Deutero-Isaiah was, in every way, a new and unique interpretation of the place and the function of the Jewish people. While certainly much of it was a product of the prophet's spiritual imagination, it was also shaped by the social conditions of the time. It would probably never have been said, much less believed or accepted, had the times not been ripe for it. Let us take a moment to look at the situation in which Deutero-Isaiah lived and preached.

Cyrus, the Agent of God

In the year 538, the Persians and the Babylonians met in battle at a place called Opis on the Tigres River. The Persian king was Cyrus. He was victorious, and a few weeks later the great capital city of Babylon fell to him without a struggle.

He became master of the middle eastern world. This was the beginning of the Persian Empire, which was to last 200 years until its destruction by the Greek, Alexander the Great.

Cyrus was one of the most enlightened rulers in human history. He respected the traditional forms of religion and culture of those people he captured. He stopped the usual practice of deporting captive populations to a foreign land and even permitted exiles to return to their lands if they chose to do so. Little wonder, then, that the leaders of the Jewish people in exile in Babylonia saw his rise to power not only as a fresh opportunity for freedom but also saw him as a heaven-sent redeemer of the Jewish faith. What for Cyrus seemed simply good practical political policy was, in Jewish eyes, a sign of some new Divine intention. To the Jewish people, Cyrus became God's instrument, a shepherd to fulfill God's purpose. It is at this point that we begin to see the genius of Deutero-Isaiah. The purpose of the end of the exile, he said, is not just to return the people to Jerusalem, there to rebuild the Temple and reestablish a new political commonwealth. The purpose of the liberation and return is no less than to help save humanity.

> And He said to me, "You are My servant,
> Israel in whom I glory."
>
> For He has said:
> "It is too little that you should be My servant
> In that I raise up the tribes of Jacob
> And restore the survivors of Israel:
> I will also make you a light of nations,
> That My salvation may reach the ends of the earth."
> Isa. 49:3,6

The salvation about which Deutero-Isaiah spoke is not of an otherworldly kind. It had nothing to do with life after death or bliss in the "next world." These ideas of being "saved," which are so much a part of the Christian world's understanding of the meaning of the world salvation, did not exist in Deutero-Isaiah's day. When he spoke of "saving," he meant literally saving people from the terrors, the misery, the poverty, the hunger, the desperate conditions of life that existed then and there in the real world. Thus Deutero-Isaiah taught that Cyrus freed the people of Israel so that they might fulfill their purpose, their mission in the world:

> I the Lord, in My grace, have summoned you,
> And I have grasped you by the hand.
> I created you, and appointed you
> A covenant-people, a light of nations—
> Opening eyes deprived of light,
> Rescuing prisoners from confinement,
> From the dungeon those who sit in darkness.
>
> Isa. 42:6–7

As a "light of nations," the people of Israel had the task of showing that the entire world is included in the Divine promise of a peaceful and just world. The prophet saw the Jewish people as being chosen by God to be God's agent; to witness, by their high ethical behavior, to the fact of God's existence.

He affirmed that God alone directs the course of history, and that God alone is the savior of all people. In the sense that Deutero-Isaiah used the word "witness," it means to "testify to." The Jewish people were to testify to the existence of the One God, the source of ethical behavior:

> My witness are *you*
>
> —declares the Lord—
>
> My servant, whom I have chosen.
> To the end that you may take thought,
> And believe in Me,
> And understand that I am He:
> Before Me no god was formed,
> And after Me none shall exist—
> None but Me, the Lord.
> Beside Me, none can grant triumph.
>
> Isa. 43:10–11

Moreover, Deutero-Isaiah challenged the nations to bring
proof that the power of their gods could in any way match
the power of God.

> Who measured the waters with the hollow of his hand,
> And gauged the skies with a span,
> And meted earth's dust with a measure,
> And weighed the mountains with a scale
> And the hills with a balance?
>
> Isa. 40:12

Implied, of course, was the answer: No other god could do
what God had done. No other god except God uses humanity and nations to fulfill the majestic plan for the future:

> Hearken to Me, My people,
> And give ear to Me, O My nation,
> For teaching shall go forth from Me,
> My way for the light of peoples.
> In a moment I will bring it:
> The triumph I grant is near,
> The success I give has gone forth.
> My arms shall provide for the peoples;
> The coastlands shall trust in Me,
> They shall look to My arm.
>
> Isa. 51:4–5

SUMMING UP

We began this chapter by asking how the Jewish people can
preserve its identity. We have tried to show how the biblical
writers, particularly the prophets, used the concept of election to answer this question. Not only did they see the idea
of chosenness as a way to help the people preserve its identity, they also saw this idea of being chosen by God as a way
to give some purpose to being Jewish. Choice became a
mission: to witness ethically to the world. Put in simple
terms, this meant that Jews were taught, or came to believe,

that if they behaved ethically, if they tried to bring justice into the world, if they expressed love, mercy, and compassion, then other peoples, seeing the positive effects of such behavior, would copy the pattern. Thus, the much prayed for "reign of righteousness" would come into being universally.

Was this too much to expect? Was it naive? Were Jews being arrogant in their expectations? Would assigning such a grand goal to one's own group make others angry, envious? Does it make any sense for modern Jews to retain so idealistic an expectation? Is there any reason why we should retain this idea of chosenness?

We will share with you our response to these difficult questions at the end of the next chapter. But before we do, it may be important to see how others, particularly Christians, understood and exploited this idea of election for their own purposes. Remember, Christianity originally sprang from Judaism. Its roots are deep in Judaism's soil. It inherited many of Judaism's ideas, ideas it could not and did not ignore. But it could and did shape that inheritance. Early Christian thinkers and writers used some of those ideas to fit their own specific needs. Sometimes that shaping affected Jews negatively. Such was particularly the case with the old prophetic idea of the Chosen People.

VI

Christianity and the Idea of Chosenness

CHRISTIANITY began in Israel five centuries after the death of the last prophet, Malachi. But the old idea of chosenness still must have been floating around in people's heads since one of the first questions early Christian thinkers addressed themselves to was: Is chosenness a condition reserved exclusively for Jews, or can other people also consider themselves chosen? Specifically, what about Christians? Are Christians also a chosen group in God's eyes?

Their answer? Yes!

They turned to history for the first justification of their answer. They saw how the Romans had conquered Israel, destroyed the Temple, and plowed Jerusalem to the ground. They saw the Jewish people exiled again from their land. Why, they asked, did that happen? Their answer: Because the Jews rejected Jesus as the Messiah. For this "sin," God punished the Jewish people with exile and the loss of their Temple. Moreover, they reasoned, for this "sin," God rejected the Jewish people. God's earlier election of the Jews had now passed over to the Christians who, as believers in the Christ, called themselves "the new people of God."

They then turned from history to the biblical writings, particularly the writings of the prophets, for further confirmation of their claim. By the second and third centuries of the common era, the writers of Christian religious thought began to interpret that earlier prophetic material as not only predicting the coming of Jesus as the Messiah, but also as suggesting that Jesus was foreseen as one who would stand in a special relationship to God.

If Judaism saw its *people* as chosen, Christianity saw that Divine choice as narrowing down to the single figure of *Jesus,* their messiah. Remember that Christians accept the truth of the Hebrew Bible. To them it is the forerunner to the New Testament which, they believe, continues and completes the Hebrew Scriptures. Understandably, Christians would want to find confirmation in the Hebrew Bible of their belief that the messiahship of Jesus was anticipated in material written as much as 750 years before his birth. Thus the writings of the prophets, particularly material found in Deutero-Isaiah, became extremely important for them. Christianity would not reject the idea of chosenness. It would, and did, merely understand and apply it differently. Christianity understood Jesus as chosen, the fulfillment of a Divine promise made at first through an ancient covenant with an ancient people from whom, they acknowledge, he sprang. Jesus, according to Christian thought, was the fulfillment of God's promise to the prophets. Prophetic figures of speech, such as "servant" and "mission," took on meanings totally different from those originally intended. Historically, these differences in interpretation caused much misunderstanding, even hatred, between Christians and Jews. Strange as it may seem to us today, it is only within the past three or four decades that many of the misunderstandings have been addressed and reduced.

DID THE PROPHETS ACTUALLY PREDICT THE COMING OF JESUS AS THE MESSIAH?

Some Christians still think so, though today most Christian and Jewish scholars would agree that none of the prophets, writing 750 years before Jesus was born, had him or anyone like him in mind when they wrote.

Why, then, and from what material do Christians seek

to establish this claim? The most commonly cited references are the so-called "servant passages" found in the writings of Deutero-Isaiah, some of which we have referred to in the previous chapter.

In at least three passages, the "servant" is described in the Hebrew Bible as a male individual, chosen by God to do God's bidding:

> This is My servant, whom I uphold,
> My chosen one, in whom I delight.
> I have put My spirit upon him,
> He shall teach the true way to the nations.
> He shall not cry out or shout aloud,
> Or make his voice heard in the streets.
> He shall not break even a bruised reed,
> Or snuff out even a dim wick.
> He shall bring forth the true way.
> He shall not grow dim or be bruised
> Till he has established the true way on earth;
> And the coastlands shall await his teaching.
>
> Isa. 42:1–4

> Listen, O coastlands, to me,
> And give heed, O nations afar:
> The Lord appointed me before I was born,
> He named me while I was in my mother's womb.
> And He said to me, "You are My servant,
> Israel in whom I glory."
>
> Isa. 49:1,3

> Indeed, My servant shall prosper,
> Be exalted and raised to great heights.
>
> He was despised, shunned by men,
> A man of suffering, familiar with disease.
> As one who hid his face from us,
> He was despised, we held him of no account.
>
> Isa. 52:13; 53:3

> Assuredly, I will give him the many as his portion,
> He shall receive the multitude as his spoil.
> For he exposed himself to death
> And was numbered among the sinners,

Whereas he bore the guilt of the many
And made intercession for sinners.

Isa. 53:12

Throughout the ages Christians have read, sung, and taught these passages to justify their belief that Jesus' birth, life, and death were all telegraphed by Judaism. Since they believe that this is the case, many Christians wonder how it is possible for Jews not to accept Jesus as the Christ.

The first thing to observe is that in the writings of Deutero-Isaiah, the servant is identified as the *people of Israel,* not as an individual. God speaks:

But you, Israel, My servant,
Jacob, whom I have chosen,
Seed of Abraham My friend—
You whom I drew from the ends of the earth
And called from its far corners,
To whom I said: You are My servant;
I chose you, I have not rejected you—
Fear not, for I am with you,
Be not frightened, for I am your God;
I strengthen you and I help you,
I uphold you with My victorious right hand.

Isa. 41:8–10

Again:

But hear, now, O Jacob My servant,
Israel whom I have chosen!
Thus said the Lord, your Maker,
Your Creator who has helped you since birth:
Fear not, My servant Jacob,
Jeshurun whom I have chosen.

Isa. 44:1–2

Remember these things, O Jacob,
For you, O Israel, are My servant:
I fashioned you, you are My servant—
O Israel, never forget Me.

Isa. 44:21

In another passage, God speaks to the conquering Cyrus, God's agent, about the chosen servant:

> For the sake of My servant Jacob,
> Israel My chosen one,
> I call you by name,
> I hail you by title, though you have not known Me.
>
> Isa. 45:4

That the servant is explicitly identified with the people of Israel is further confirmed by Deutero-Isaiah, in the verse:

> And He said to me, "You are My servant,
> Israel in whom I glory."
>
> Isa. 49:3

Deutero-Isaiah wanted the people to understand that they had an active role to play in redeeming the world. It is not God's work alone.

Today most biblical scholars agree that the servant about whom the prophet wrote was not an individual, certainly not one who was to be born six centuries later, but the Jewish people who lived then, in the prophet's day, and who, as we have seen, Deutero-Isaiah believed had a special mission to perform.

THE SUFFERING SERVANT: DIFFERING VIEWS

A further point of serious disagreement between Jewish and Christian understandings of prophetic writing is in the so-called "suffering servant" passages of Deutero-Isaiah. Chapter 53, verses 2–9, particularly speak of one "despised, shunned by men, a man of suffering, familiar with disease." The imagery continues:

As one who hid his face from us,
He was despised, we held him of no account.
Yet it was our sickness that he was bearing,
Our suffering that he endured.
We accounted him plagued,
Smitten and afflicted by God;
But he was wounded because of our sins,
Crushed because of our iniquities.
He bore the chastisement that made us whole,
And by his bruises we were healed.
We all went astray like sheep,
Each going his own way;
And the Lord visited upon him
The guilt of all of us.

He was maltreated, yet he was submissive,
He did not open his mouth;
Like a sheep being led to slaughter,
Like a ewe, dumb before those who shear her,
He did not open his mouth.
By oppressive judgment he was taken away,
Who could describe his abode?
For he was cut off from the land of the living
Through the sin of My people, who deserved the punishment.
And his grave was set among the wicked,
And with the rich, in his death—
Though he had done no injustice
And had spoken no falsehood.

Historically, Christians saw these as clear prophetic references to Jesus, whom they claimed suffered precisely as was described and was God's chosen servant. Verses such as these became "proof texts" that Jesus was not only God's suffering servant, but that he had indeed died for the sins of humanity.

Judaism sees both the meaning and the context of these words quite differently. Remember, one of the central features of Deutero-Isaiah's message was the prediction that a new age was about to dawn on the earth. Cyrus's rise to power was a signal of the approach of that new age. The people of Israel, God's servant, was to help bring the message of this new age, a message of hope and peace, to the ends of the earth [and the "coastlands shall await his teaching"]. God had tested and refined the lives of the people of Israel with the suffering and punishment of the exile. That would now be over. The punishment of the exile was completed and finished, a thing of the past. The suffering that the people had endured by being uprooted from their land was about to end. The people stood now in the dawn of a new day. Thus the servant is a figure representing past suffering and future hope. These suffering-servant passages speak not of a people destined *to* suffer, but of a people who *has* suffered. All the verbs in the verses are in the past tense: "So marred *was* his appearance" (Isa. 52:14). "He *was* despised" (Isa. 53:3). But the pain and suffering has ended. The future will be far better:

> Indeed, My servant shall prosper,
> Be exalted and raised to great heights.
>
> Isa. 52:13

Such is the Jewish understanding of the suffering servant.

One can easily see how wide the gulf was between the two faiths in their differing understandings of chosenness. That difference made for much trouble between them.

By the fourth century of the common era, Christianity became the official religion of the Roman Empire. Christians had begun to see themselves as "the new Israel" and "the newly chosen," displacing the "old." The effect of this Christian self-understanding was devastating for the Jews. If God had now chosen the newly elect rather than the old, then, Christians reasoned, it was necessary to bring all people, Jews included, to an acceptance of Jesus as the Christ. Jews, however, refused to accept this logic or its consequences. This led Christianity to consider the Jewish people as betrayers of a sacred trust, the fulfillment of their own notion of election. The church leaders reasoned that the old covenant was dissolved. Since the Jews had rejected "God," now God had rejected *them.* The church proclaimed the old law—the Torah—dead, its people replaced.

But the Jewish people continued to live, to practice the "dead" law as though it were alive and possessed of meaning. Their very presence in history was a denial of the claim of Christianity. As the church grew in power, it felt it could not allow that denial to stand, and so Christianity began a campaign of either converting or oppressing this stubborn remnant, a witness to their own "blindness." The story of Christian persecution of the Jewish people from the fourth century to modern times is well-known. We shall not detail it here. It explains another reason why the idea of chosenness survived. The more Jews found themselves oppressed for their faith, the more they clung to their faith for inner strength. To be sure, there were some who, with bitterness and pessimism, questioned: Were the Jews chosen for persecution? How long must we wait for the messianic moment?

The history of Jewish life from the middle ages until the nineteenth century, the time of intellectual enlightenment and political emancipation, is a history of how the Jewish people struggled to find answers to those two questions, and the ways of thought and action Jews developed in order to survive, while awaiting a better day. The more we were insulted, the more we needed something to give us a sense of worth—not superiority, just worth. That something was the idea of being chosen. At least it gave some reason for the pain of persecution. In the end, it was not religious enlightenment that freed Jews from ghettos or from the attacks of spiritually enflamed mobs. What finally brought freedom and a measure of toleration to the Jewish people were the new areas of secular knowledge and political freedom. They began to weaken the effects of traditional Christian thinking and to change Christian-Jewish relations for the better. For example, we are living today in a time when the Roman Catholic church has changed its attitude about the election of Jewish people. As a result, the church has changed its approach to the Jews. At the last great convocation of the bishops and leaders of the church, held in Rome in 1965, the Vatican issued a famous document, *On the Relation of the Church to the Jewish People.* In it there is an important sentence which reads:

> . . . God holds the Jews most dear for the sake of the Fathers; His gift and call are irrevocable.

VATICAN REVISION

This small sentence represents an enormous change in official church thinking. It is a recognition, based on an interpretation of a statement of Paul's found in the New Testament (Rom. 11:1) that the covenant between the people of Israel and God, who chose them, is an eternal covenant. It follows then that Christianity could never be seen as replacing Judaism.

We see here a recognition by the church of the vitality of Judaism and the Jewish people. The document goes on to say:

> Since the spiritual patrimony common to Christians and Jews is so great, the Council wants to foster and recommend a mutual knowledge and respect which is the fruit above all of biblical and theological studies, as well as of fraternal dialogue.

In the years since the issuance of that historic document, the Roman Catholic church has tried to fulfill its goal. In 1975, the church issued a set of guidelines for their religious community, which stressed the importance of ongoing contact with Jews all over the world. This has greatly opened up Catholic-Jewish contact. Catholics are now learning about Judaism and they are learning, some for the first time, the history of their church's oppression of the Jewish people.

In 1977, a brilliant Catholic scholar gave a paper before a small group of Catholics and Jews, all of whom were official representatives of their religious communities. There he clearly demonstrated that it was wrong for the church to seek the conversion of the Jews, and that such an approach was historically not justifiable. The mission of the church, he said, is not to witness *to* the Jews (that is, to seek their conversion), but to join *with* the Jewish people in a mission to the world, to seek to bring justice and peace to humanity, which is in desperate need of these qualities. It is a new position for the Roman Catholic church, and it comes out of a reinterpretation of the very, very old idea of chosenness.

Not all of Christianity has adopted this enlightened view. There are still some elements of Christianity, especially some rather aggressive Jewish-Christians, who have made Jews their special target for missionary efforts. Most of these groups, like Jews for Jesus, Beth Saar Shalom, The Way, and others, are not part of what we call mainstream Protestant church groups, like the Episcopalians, Methodists, or Presbyterians. They are, in fact, something of an embarrassment to these groups. These missionaries to the Jews take the words of the Bible very literally. They are not much interested in the historical development of the ideas we have explored above. They believe they have a mission to bring all people to the acceptance of Jesus as Christ, especially Jews, since Jesus came from the Jewish community. They misuse Jewish symbols and ritual items like the *talit,* kiddush cup, Shabbat, and holidays to appeal to Jews, particularly young Jews. In some instances, they use people who were born Jews, but who have become Christians, to testify to their beliefs to a Jewish population. Some groups even use brainwashing, deception, and fraud to ensnare Jews into their faiths.

How should we Jews respond? Some Jews would like to get the courts to stop them. But aren't these people legally entitled to practice their religion, as we are to practice Judaism? What do you think?

Are these aggressive missionary sects morally correct? In what ways?

We shall return to these questions in our next chapter, when we discuss Jewish identity. In the meantime, it is important to see just how compelling an idea like chosenness can become, and to what difficulties, even suffering, it has led and can lead. In light of this, we are forced to ask, "Does anyone today really need such an old idea?" Given the separation it has caused between groups, as well as the anguish it has brought the Jewish people, would it be better to drop the idea altogether? Is there any modern value to continuing to think of ourselves as chosen?

THE MODERN APPLICATION OF ELECTION

There was a time when many Jews were convinced that the idea of being a chosen people was as embarrassing as it was outdated. One very distinguished modern American rabbi, Mordecai Kaplan, taught that the Chosen People idea is not in harmony with our modern lives, it is an idea that lingers on but has no present meaning or purpose.

> The idea of Israel as the Chosen People must, therefore, be understood as belonging to a thought world we no longer inhabit. . . . The very notion that a people can for all time be the elect of God implies an epic or dramatic conception of history, a history predetermined in form and aim. Nowadays for any people to call itself "chosen" is to be guilty of self-infatuation.
>
> Mordecai Kaplan, *The Future of the American Jew,* p. 211

Moreover, at one time, Reform Judaism tried to eradicate the whole idea of being a chosen people from its teachings. It even went so far as to eliminate all references to the Jews as a chosen people from its prayerbooks. Our early Reformers *chose* to be *unchosen*.

Some Jews, particularly before the period of World War II, chose not to be chosen for reasons different from those suggested by Dr. Kaplan. They wished to drop their Jewish identity altogether. Those Jews who tried to melt into the general culture often changed their Jewish-sounding names to more American-, English-, French-, or German-sounding names. Some who felt that their physical features looked "too Jewish" even went so far as to try to change their noses or other features. Many disdained Hebrew and refused to teach it to their children. Some abandoned all Jewish laws regarding food or observance of the holy days and holidays. In short, they tried to assimilate (disappear) into the larger society. Tragically, they learned from Hitler that this could not be done very successfully, and they learned from the postwar period that it was not necessary or desirable. Instead of cutting themselves off from their ancestral roots, people after World War II began to search for identity and to define themselves in terms of their roots. We entered into a period of pluralism, where being different was important and respected. We have learned again that people can't be anybody without an identity, and that our religious, historical, and cultural past is part of what gives people an identity. Universalism should not mean loss of individual or group identity. Uniforms give an athletic team a group identity. Flags give a people a national identity. Religious beliefs and practices give a people a spiritual identity.

IS BEING JEWISH A WORTHWHILE VALUE FOR TODAY'S WORLD?

But doesn't the insistence on ethnic and racial identity cause conflict among peoples, as in the conflict between the Jews and Moslems in the Middle East, or Catholics and Protestants in Northern Ireland today?

Can one preserve and nurture one's racial or ethnic identity and still be a universalist, interested in and actively involved in the causes of humanity?

I look at the world and I look at the Jew. Despite all its
political diversity and the persistence of force and struggle,
I see a world drifting toward ever increasing conformity of
spirit, habit, thought and behavior. I see the Jew desperately maintaining his identity, often without apparent purpose, often instinctively. Often he is ignorant of his past
and ignorant even of the possibilities of meaning that his
present might hold for him. Often he merely exists, yet
here too he may be serving a purpose beyond himself. For
in the sea of conformity he may be the rock of difference.
Perhaps it is the destiny of the Jew today to maintain the
possibility of minority and diversity.

> Gunther G. Plaut,
> *The Case for the Chosen People,* p. 120

Do you subscribe to that view? Do you see any value in it?
Why, or why not?

Some believe we must retain our sense of chosenness in
order to carry our social ideas to the world. A healthy society
is good for Jews. Jewish security is linked to the well-being
of the larger community. It is in the Jewish self-interest to
work for the freedom and welfare of all people. That is our
mission as a people. In the well-being of all humanity, we
find our own security.

LIVING IT TODAY

One last question: Assuming that there are some Jews,
young and old, who believe in the value of maintaining the
chosenness of their Jewish identity and who wish to give it
expression, how do they go about doing that? How do people
live their belief that they are members of a chosen people?

Certainly not by acting in a proud or arrogant way. That
is a denial of everything the concept ever meant. Nor by
making Judaism an exclusive club. Chosenness was not
meant to exclude anyone. Everyone can be a chosen person
if he or she chooses to be so. The election of Israel does not

preclude the election of others. All who commit themselves to the ethical and moral demands of Torah can claim to be chosen. Anyone who wishes to embrace Judaism, and its mitzvot, can join the Jewish faith and people.

The first way to express chosenness is by making a commitment to know as much as possible about the mitzvot, folkways, and history of Judaism. Without such knowledge, we will be cut off from the foundations of the covenant. The rabbis were right when they said, "An ignorant person cannot be pious."

Also, our lives must reflect some Jewish discipline, be it what we eat and do not eat, our loyalty to the Jewish people, or our worship experiences. There are Jewish deeds to do. That, too, is part of being a covenant people.

Finally, our lives must express deeds of service to the larger community. Covenanted Jews will seek the welfare of the community and strive, at every opportunity, to enrich it. Wherever Jews have lived in an atmosphere of freedom, they have been prominent in efforts for better education, human rights, social justice, more humane health conditions, and social welfare. These are the ways we have expressed our commitment to mission, and these are the ways we must continue to do so.

It is not an easy task. But the great German writer, Heinrich Heine, was right when he said, "Jews are just like other people, only more so."

VII

Ritual and Prayer

DEBBIE was just plain bored. The Rosh Hashanah service was so dull. But she had enjoyed the shofar service. The sound of that horn always stimulated her imagination, and besides, it was a break in the otherwise unchanging routine of responsive reading. The rabbi's droning and the choir's music sounded to her as if they were coming from somewhere inside an echo chamber. "Why do smart, grown-up people do this all the time?" The thought kept nagging her. "Worse, why do they make *us* do it too?"

She kept looking at her watch, fiddling, fidgeting. She wished she'd brought a magazine and slipped it into the prayerbook. At least she'd have something to read. But she guessed her parents probably wouldn't let her read it anyway. They were scowling at her again. What a bore!

When the rabbi said, "And now we will continue on page so and so," Debbie would mechanically turn the pages of the book and half-scan the words. She hardly understood them anyway. No one really talked like that. What does it all mean? What good is it? And who needs it anyway?

She was deep into her own thoughts about the upcoming football game, only half-listening, when she heard the rabbi exclaim:

> Bringing oblations is futile,
> Incense is offensive to Me.

New moon and sabbath,
Proclaiming of solemnities,
Assemblies with iniquity,
I cannot abide.
Your new moons and fixed seasons
Fill Me with loathing;
They are become a burden to Me,
I cannot endure them.

Debbie suddenly began to pay attention. She looked at the prayerbook to see what the rabbi was reading. There it was, in plain sight. "Who wrote that?" she asked herself, "and why is it in the prayerbook on Rosh Hashanah? It doesn't matter, whoever wrote it was right. Now you're talking," she thought. "That's just the way I feel. All this ritual junk is just that—junk!"

Debbie couldn't wait to confront her religious school teacher with this one. She had discovered something. She had discovered that someone important enough to be included in the prayerbook had said that prayer and sacrifice are not what God wants, and if that's true, why did she have to go to services? You can't force someone to pray. What's the big deal about praying?

What Debbie didn't know was that the rabbi had been reading a quotation from the first chapter of the prophet Isaiah. The entire section (chapter 1, verses 10 through 17) is a powerful condemnation of ritual. Debbie also didn't know that this rejection of ritual is found in the writings of other prophets. Amos, for example, said the same thing in even stronger language:

I loathe, I spurn your festivals,
I am not appeased by your solemn assemblies.

Spare Me the sound of your hymns,
And let Me not hear the music of your lutes.

Amos 5:21, 23

He even became very sarcastic in his denunciation of ritual:

> Come to Bethel and transgress;
> To Gilgal, and transgress even more:
> Present your sacrifices the next morning
> And your tithes on the third day;
> And burn a thank offering of leavened bread;
> And proclaim freewill offerings loudly.
> For you love that sort of thing, O Israelites
>   —declares my Lord God.
>   Amos 4:4–5

Micah, who lived about the same time as Amos and Isaiah, was equally scornful of the people's belief that they were acting in a religious way by bringing sacrifices to the Temple:

> With what shall I approach the Lord,
> Do homage to God on high?
> Shall I approach Him with burnt offerings,
> With calves a year old?
> Would the Lord be pleased with thousands of rams,
> With myriads of streams of oil?
> Shall I give my firstborn for my transgression,
> The fruit of my body for my sins?
>
> He has told you, O man, what is good,
> And what the Lord requires of you:
> Only to do justice
> And to love goodness,
> And to walk modestly with your God.
>   Mic. 6:6–8

Jeremiah was likewise disgusted with what was obviously a widespread belief that going through the ritual practice of bringing sacrifices to the Temple was the way to worship God.

> What need have I of frankincense
> That comes from Sheba,
> Or fragrant cane from a distant land?

Your burnt offerings are not acceptable
And your sacrifices are not pleasing to Me.

Jer. 6:20

In his famous Temple sermon, probably delivered at the moment when the newly appointed king of Israel, Jehoiakim, was about to receive his crown in the Temple in Jerusalem, Jeremiah boldly attacked the entire ritual cult:

> Don't put your trust in illusions and say, "The Temple of the Lord, the Temple of the Lord, the Temple of the Lord are these [buildings]."
>
> Will you steal and murder and commit adultery and swear falsely, and sacrifice to Baal, and follow other gods whom you have not experienced, and then come and stand before Me in this House which bears My name and say, "We are safe"?—[Safe to do all these abhorrent things!]
>
> Thus said the Lord of Hosts, the God of Israel: Add your burnt offerings to your other sacrifices and eat the meat! For when I freed your fathers from the land of Egypt, I did not speak with them or command them concerning burnt offerings or sacrifice.

Jer. 7:4, 9–10, 21–22

Even Ezekiel, who was a priest as well as a prophet (see Ezek. 1:3), attacked the very ritual practices which he was consecrated to maintain and which, after all, provided him with his livelihood. It was as if a rabbi told the congregation from the pulpit that prayer was a waste of time. Yet Ezekiel preached that God was revolted by the people's behavior, and so would allow the destruction of the Temple:

> I am going to desecrate My Sanctuary, your pride and glory, the delight of your eyes and the desire of your heart; and the sons and daughters you have left behind shall fall by the sword.

Ezek. 24:21

What do we learn from all this? Simply that all the prophets who lived in Israel before the destruction of the country, first by the Assyrians and later by the Babylonians, seemed to be fiercely against ritual.

What do you think the Jewish community of America would do if all the rabbis and leading thinkers of this community were suddenly to issue a public statement saying that worship as conducted in the synagogues was not what God wanted, but indeed something that God actually hated? That is exactly the impression we get of the attitude the preexilic prophets seemed to express about the sacrificial cult, the way of worshipping God that was practiced in those days.

Were the prophets really against ritual? If so, what did they want in its place? Is ritual at all important? Is there any value to prayer and worship? Is there a difference between these two? Can people live without ritual?

The prophets of Israel made a distinction between means and ends. A means is a technique, the way we achieve a goal. An end is the goal we seek to achieve.

Were the prophets against rituals? Yes, if seen as ends in themselves. No, if understood as means (techniques) by which to achieve a greater end (an understanding of what God really wanted people to do). Organized prayer as a means by which to become conscious of God did not exist in the days of those prophets who lived *before* the Babylonian exile. The earliest forms by which people worshipped the gods (or God) was by bringing something tangible to a special place dedicated to the god. The place could be a grove of trees, a stand of rocks, a mountain top, an especially beautiful pond, lake, or river. These were often called "high places"; later they were called "shrines." In time, people built structures and, later, buildings to give a sense of permanence and greater importance to the place; they appointed men (and sometimes women) to keep the place. They would call such people priests or priestesses and usually endowed them with special powers and privileges.

Primitive people did not always understand the natural world around them. They feared what they did not know (many people are still afraid of the dark), and sought to appease the forces in the world that they saw as very powerful so that these forces would not destroy them, their homes, their crops, their cattle, or other valued possessions. Very often people brought gifts to calm the gods they associated with the elements. If a high place was designated as a place dedicated to a god associated with some aspect of agriculture, people might bring gifts of grain, or cereals. If such a spot became a place dedicated to a god of the herds and flocks, people might bring a lamb, ram, or cow, slaughter it there, and offer it to the god. It is likely that they would even eat a little of this sacrifice to associate themselves with the god being addressed. This is how the practice of sacrifice started. For thousands of years it was *the only known form* of addressing an object considered to be divine. For Judaism it was the only known form of addressing God from the time of Abraham (about 1,800 years before the common era) to the time of the Babylonian exile.

Since the Babylonians destroyed the Temple in Jerusalem, which had by that time become the center of the sacrificial system, it is likely that other ways of addressing God, such as prayer and worship, developed at that time. But when the Temple in Jerusalem was rebuilt, the practice of bringing *things* to the Temple, and there sacrificing them to God, was resumed and remained in force until the year 70 C.E., when the Romans destroyed the Temple for all times. By the time of the great prophets, the system of sacrifice had become very complicated and was highly organized. The system was centered around the Temple in Jerusalem (first built by King Solomon about 955 B.C.E.), but it had been in existence for hundreds of years before that time. The Bible is filled with the details of sacrifice (see Exod. 29–30; Lev. 1–9; Deut. 12:5–7). By the time of the prophets, the practice was as commonly accepted by the Israelites as the way to worship God, as we, today, accept the synagogue as the place to pray.

The prophets did not seem to object to the rite of sacrificing in the Temple or at other places throughout the land, but they objected to people's thinking that this was the only requirement God made of them as a religious demand. Sacrifice, to the prophets, could not be a substitute for doing justice, being honest, or showing kindness or mercy. Sacrifice was to be seen only as a means to this greater end. In other words, it could not become an end in itself. It was a technique by which people would better understand what God really wanted of the people. Sacrifice was the magnifying glass through which the people could see more clearly the *ethical demands* that God placed on the people. That is why commands for just behavior immediately follow each of the condemnations of sacrifice.

After Isaiah says that God cannot endure the sacrificial ceremonies built up as solemn assemblies around such sacred times as the appearance of the new moon or the coming of the Sabbath, he immediately goes on to say that what God wants the people to do is:

> Wash yourselves clean;
> Put your evil doings
> Away from My sight.
> Cease to do evil;
> Learn to do good.
> Devote yourselves to justice;
> Aid the wronged.
> Uphold the rights of the orphan;
> Defend the cause of the widow.
>
> Isa. 1:16–17

When Micah says that God is not pleased with the sacrifice of even a thousand rams, he follows instantly with a statement describing what would really please God:

> He has told you, O man, what is good,
> And what the Lord requires of you:
> Only to do justice

And to love goodness,
And to walk modestly with your God.

Mic. 6:8

Similarly when Amos is finished telling the people that God rejects all their sacrificial gifts, he concludes by telling the people:

> But let justice well up like water,
> Righteousness like an unfailing stream.

Amos 5:24

The prophets of Israel would have agreed with those who criticize organized religion for ignoring the social ills of their communities. Recent surveys show that more than half of the members of religious institutions believe that it is not the function of their synagogues and churches to become involved in or speak out on matters of social justice.

Do you think these people are right?

What about the attitude of those who believe that both the expression of ritual and the doing of social justice are important functions of a synagogue or church? Consider the following statement:

> Religion cannot be indifferent to social justice but neither can its major task be equated with its pursuit. The primary role of religion is . . . (to provide) a ritual and mystic structure in which the abiding realities of life and death can be shared. As long as men are born, pass through the crises of transition in life, experience guilt, fail—as fail they must—grow old, and die, traditional churches and synagogues will be irreplaceable institutions.
>
> Richard Rubenstein, *After Auschwitz:*
> *Radical Theology and Contemporary Judaism,*
> Bobbs Merrill Co., Inc., 1966, pp. 205–206

A Protestant thinker, Harvey Cox, said the same thing this way:

> Once you transform everything into a mission for social
> action and lose the intrinsic joy of the spirit of worship, you
> are in danger of losing both . . . You don't really worship
> and you don't really serve.
>
> *Time,* March 15, 1968, p. 53

No one before the prophets had ever told the people that
sacrifice was a means, and not an end in and of itself, or that
the purpose of sacrifice was only to help the people to focus
more clearly on God's ethical demands. In this, the prophets
added something brand new to the people's understanding
of religion. Were they opposed to ritual? Not really. But they
were deeply opposed to letting sacrifice become the end-all
and the be-all of religion.

So far we have tried to show how the prophets who
lived before the Babylonian exile felt about the place of
ritual in religion. They spoke this way not only because they
honestly believed that religion demanded more of people
than simply performing certain prescribed rituals, but also
because they were convinced that a failure by the people to
really do justice would so anger God that God would break
the covenant with them and punish them for their failure.

As matters developed, their concern seemed to be justified. By the year 586 B.C.E., the stronger nations surrounding Israel had subdivided and conquered her. Babylonians
had taken the remnant of the Jewish people into exile. Naturally the people demanded to know why.

Either the preexilic prophets were clever enough to see
that other nations surrounding Israel were militarily more
powerful than Israel and about to conquer her, or they simply believed that God would no longer protect the Jewish
people because of their violation of their end of the contract.
The prophets provided a powerful answer to those who
asked why, if God is supposed to be our protector, were we
being overwhelmed by the surrounding nations. They said
that the people were punished because they had mixed up
ends and means. Assyria and Babylon would capture and

control the people of Israel precisely because the Jewish people had failed to understand that God wanted those who called themselves religious to be both ethical and ritually observant. The bringing of sacrifices is only a means, never an end in itself. In effect, the prophets saved God for the people. Had it not been for the prophets' message, the people might have come to believe that their God was not what the founders of the Jewish religion had said God was: All Powerful, God of gods. The northern Kingdom of Israel was conquered by the Assyrians, not because God was weak, but because the people had not acted justly or sought righteousness. Therefore God allowed Assyria to take Israel captive. God used Assyria as a punishing instrument. Isaiah said it most dramatically:

> Ha!
> Assyria, rod of My anger,
> In whose hand, as a staff, is My fury!
> I send him against an ungodly nation,
> I charge him against a people that provokes Me,
> To take its spoil and to seize its booty
> And to make it a thing trampled
> Like the mire of the streets.
>
> Isa. 10:5–6

The prophets both of and after the exile were not quite as outspoken against ritual. There was no reason to be. The situation was different and it called for a different response. If the Jewish community of Judah had asked why this happened to us, afterward they asked, "Now, how shall we live?"

Jeremiah, who lived both before and during the exile, told the people to be patient and to wait. Until now, the Hebrew people believed that their God was limited to the land of Canaan (Palestine), and that it was only there that God could be worshipped. With the exile, Jeremiah introduced a new idea. God was not tied to any one place. God was the God of the entire universe. God could be found everywhere and, therefore, could be worshipped anywhere. One did not need a Temple in Jerusalem or shrines in Bethel or Ai. Therefore, Jeremiah told his fellow Jews in exile to plant vineyards in Babylon, to establish homes and families in exile, to be loyal to the government, to seek God with a full heart, and to be patient. He counselled them not to give up their belief in God, nor to give up hope. (See Jer. 29:4–14.)

With the Temple in Jerusalem destroyed, sacrifice could no longer be practiced. That had always been restricted to the Temple. And yet the people had a need to do something to express their faith. Does that sound strange or unreasonable? Imagine what would happen if your school prevented all opportunities for students to come together to express their feelings about the way the school was being run, or to encourage the school's athletic teams. Imagine that your town closed all places like the corner store or local hamburger shop and kept its youth from coming together to meet and talk with one another. What do you think would happen? It wouldn't take long for young people to find secret or hidden meeting places.

Similarly, what if those who oppose religion decided to close down the synagogues and churches and to abolish all forms of ritual? How long do you think it would be until small groups of believers gathered in new places and began to develop some ritual form? Probably not very long. People seem to need to come together to express values they share. That happened in Babylonia. The people sought to replace the practices of Jerusalem by coming together informally on special days like Shabbat and holy days to give each other support and encouragement. The prophet Ezekiel encouraged that practice. These were not planned worship meetings, but it is likely that they read parts of their historic literature, especially words of hope and comfort. These meetings may have been the frame on which the structure of later worship services was built.

In 533 B.C.E. the Persian king, Cyrus, conquered the

Babylonians. Those Jews living in Babylon who wished to return to Jerusalem were permitted to do so. Most remained, but some did go back. Under the urging of prophets like Haggai and Zechariah, and with the help of Cyrus—who gave them back the gold and silver which the Babylonian king, Nebuchadnezzar, had taken away in 586 B.C.E.—a rather small Temple was finally rebuilt in Jerusalem. It wasn't easy, and it took seventeen years to finish. There the sacrificial cult was restored. The returned community was as poor as it was small, and the quality of sacrificial ritual left much to be desired. Malachi, the last of the literary prophets, complained bitterly about the way ceremonies were carried out in the Temple:

> You offer defiled food on My altar. But you ask, "How have we defiled You?" By saying, "The table of the Lord can be treated with scorn."
>
> Mal. 1:7

> When you present a blind animal for sacrifice—it doesn't matter! When you present a lame or sick one—it doesn't matter! Just offer it to your governor: Will he accept you? Will he show you favor?—said the Lord of Hosts.
>
> Mal. 1:8

The priests in the Temple "made the many stumble through your rulings" (Mal. 2:8). Intermarriage increased; nevertheless, the cult continued. But the practice of worship separate from sacrifice, which had grown in exile, spread outside of Jerusalem. It was to be the technique which eventually saved Judaism.

THE NEW WAY

Prayer replaced sacrifice as the Jewish way of worship only after the Roman conquest of Israel and the final destruction of the Temple in the year 70 C.E. We have been using prayer and worship as the way to focus on God's demands ever since, for the past 2,000 years. If the great Hebrew prophets were alive today, would they rage against prayer or public worship? Yes, if they thought people used prayer as an end itself. No, if they saw that people who prayed or worshipped used these actions to stimulate them to more ethical and sensitive behavior, and to prevent them from acting in hurtful, cruel, or destructive ways. That is one value of prayer or worship. Prayer is the mirror which can help us to see ourselves for what we are and are not.

Deutero-Isaiah knew this. During the exile, two forces dominated his thinking: the despair of the people, and the growing strength of the Persians (also known as Medes) to the east of Babylon. Whether by keen political insight or by divine inspiration, he knew that the Persians would conquer Babylon.

Deutero-Isaiah was convinced that God had sent King Cyrus to deliver the people of Israel from the hands of Babylonia. He challenged his depressed community to take heart, for the time of its exile was soon to end:

> Comfort, oh comfort My people,
> Says your God,
> Speak tenderly to Jerusalem,
> And declare to her
> That her term of service is over,
> That her iniquity is expiated;
> For she has received at the hand of the Lord
> Double for all her sins.
>
> Isa. 40:1–2

Can you imagine what these words must have meant to the Jewish people in exile? Have you ever wanted to hear comforting words from someone close and dear to you?

Prayer can do many things. Sometimes the knowledge that someone is praying for you, thinking of you, can give you courage. It is a profound form of companionship.

PRAYER IN THE SYNAGOGUE

One of Debbie's questions remains: Do we need houses of worship? Do we need a structure of ritual filled with spoken prayers, books of prayers, organ music, choirs, rabbis, and robes in order to pray or worship?

First, let us distinguish between prayer and worship. *Prayer* is what an individual does alone. *Worship* is what we call prayer done in a group. One person doesn't need all of the items mentioned above in order to pray. One can pray anytime, anywhere, whenever a situation arises that makes one feel like praying (such as a moment of crisis or of great relief). Prayer usually occurs when most of the religious trappings are absent. But prayer usually becomes more meaningful with the presence of—and in the midst of—a community. Communal prayer, called *worship,* can and frequently does help a person express emotions, including a sense of solidarity with one's own group.

All of us have watched an athletic event, concert, or movie on television. Yet why is it sometimes so hard to get a ticket to the stadium, ball park, concert hall, or theater to see one of these things in person? Why do people want to go to the place where one of these events is taking place instead of being content to see it for free, from the comfort of one's living room? The answer is both simple and complicated. First, by being there, where the event is actually taking place, there is sometimes a contagious excitement that is transmitted from person to person in a group. That enthusiasm is usually missing when one experiences these situations alone. Also, by being there with others, the quality of the experience is intensified and heightened. A great concert heard in a concert hall is more thrilling, more inspiring, more moving when shared with thousands of like-minded persons at the scene than it is when heard alone on the radio.

The same can be true of worship. People seem better able to express their emotions when they are with others

gathered in a place for the same purpose. That may be one
of the reasons why traditional Judaism insists that ten people
(a *minyan*) be present before a public religious service
(called *tefilah*) can be started. The rabbis knew that there
was a spirit engendered when worshippers came together.
Worship joins the individual Jew to the community of the
Jewish people—of the past as well as of the present.

One of the problems Reform Jewish worship once had
was that many people felt it did not give them a sufficient
opportunity to express their deepest feelings. Debbie
(whom we described at the beginning of this chapter) had
an instinctive feeling that too much was being done *for* her
and too little was being left for her to do in the synagogue
service. She was being talked *to* by the rabbi, sung *at* by the
choir. What she needed was an opportunity to do these
things herself: to sing the prayers herself, to speak more of
the words, to read and study the Torah text in the setting of
the service. She needed to express herself emotionally, to be
a part of—and not *apart from*—the service. Debbie had a
fair criticism. Worship can be boring if the worshipper is
only a passive spectator to what is going on. That is why
some congregations are now trying to get away from large
impersonal services with hidden choirs and remote rabbis,
and are turning to the smaller, more intimate worship
groups where leaders use simple musical instruments like
guitars to help the worshippers sing, even dance, and to pray
with feeling. That is one reason why people form small
chavurot in their temples. Do you think the prophets would
approve of such experiences? Do such services have greater
value and meaning? Would Debbie complain less in such a
setting?

Many Reform Jews, including young people who have
been touched by dynamic Jewish camp experiences, are
seeking to deepen their Jewish identity and to search for
their Jewish roots. Many are choosing rituals from Jewish
tradition which have particular meaning for them. Some
pray daily. Some wear *kippot* (skull caps). Some use a talit

(prayer shawl) for prayer. Some refuse to eat certain foods
(ham or seafood, for example) so as to develop a daily discipline. Many recite the *Motzi* (the blessing over bread) before every meal and sing the *Birkat Hamazon* (blessing after
the meal). Many families have introduced the lovely Hav-
dalah service to usher out the Shabbat and many have en-
riched their own Shabbat home services. Reform Jews are
free to choose which, if any, of these practices are meaningful to them. It would be tragic if these rituals were used as
a substitute for good deeds. But we now know that a good
Jew can serve God by finding joy in ritual and ceremony,
and also by fulfilling the ethical demands of the Jewish way
of life. It is, simply, not a matter of either / or—it is both / and!

VIII

Identity and Understanding

THE two series that commanded the attention of the largest viewing audiences in the recent history of American television were "Roots" and the nine-and-a-half hour special, "Holocaust." It is estimated that over 150 million viewers saw all or part of the first "Roots" series, and that 120 million watched all or part of "Holocaust."

Most analysts agreed that a major reason why so many people watched was because an increasing number of Americans want to know more about who and what they are. They are searching for their own racial, ethnic, religious, and cultural identities. So popular is this search now that an advertising campaign of one of the world's largest international airlines promoted the idea that people have two homes, one here and one somewhere else, outside of America—the place from which their parents or grandparents came. They urged Americans to go back to their ancestral homes; flying, of course, on their airline.

"Roots" gave black Americans a sense of pride, not only by showing that they have a unique history with roots that go deep into Africa, but also by portraying them as having a long history on this continent. One of the messages of "Roots" was that blacks belong here, that they have been here as long, if not longer, than most white Americans. Why doesn't a black person forget about being a part of the black race? Blacks would laugh at you for such a question. They'll tell you that they couldn't even if they wanted to; the world wouldn't let them. Besides, they don't want to. Being black is central to their identity, to what they are. To deny their blackness is to deny their essence, their personality. Besides, they are proud of their black heritage. They are part of the destiny of the black race and they want to play their part. If the world cannot accept them because of their color, the world is to be pitied. They will not become "Uncle Toms" or betray their people. Isn't that what "Roots" was all about?

Similarly, "Holocaust" reinforced in Jews a pride in being Jewish. But it also did more. The portrayal of the brutal, senseless persecution and eventual destruction of the Jewish population of Europe by Hitler gave Jewish survivors a determination to remain identifiably Jewish, even as it showed the non-Jewish world the catastrophic horror to which mindless anti-Semitism can lead. Black people came away from viewing "Roots" saying to themselves, "I am proud to be black." Jews study the Holocaust and say to themselves, "I am proud to be Jewish." The indignities and oppressions both groups have been forced to endure strengthen the will to remain a culturally, spiritually iden-tifiable group.

While people have always wanted to know who and what they are, there was a time in America when asserting one's cultural, ethnic, religious, even racial identity was not popular. It ran against the grain of the American "melting pot" dream. Until World War II, the ideal image projected for America was one of sameness, not difference. Americans were taught that, while most of us came from someplace else, the goal was to fashion a new society; and to do that we ought to be as alike as possible. As a result, first- and second-generation immigrants to these shores tried desperately to "Americanize"—to drop their old-world ties and cultures. Ethnic groups cut themselves off from their cultural and linguistic ties; some Jews tried to assimilate by dropping their religious practices and particular identities. (Unbeliev-able as it may sound, some blacks tried physically to whiten their skin and to straighten their hair.)

World War II put an end to most of that. If Americans went to war as a melting pot, they returned as members of specific groups. The history of America for the past generation has been a history of people trying to recover their past and their roots. As one sociologist observed, what the grandfathers tried to forget, the grandchildren try to remember.

JONAH

Throughout history one can find countless examples of people struggling through what has been called an "identity crisis." The reluctant prophet Jonah was a classic example of a person engaged in such a struggle. His problem was the reverse of those who sought to assimilate. He was a Hebrew who had contempt for anyone who was not. He thought he was part of a superior group, and he looked down at people who didn't belong, who were different. And so, according to the legend in the biblical book that bears his name, when God ordered him to go to the great Assyrian city of Nineveh to urge the people there to repent, he resisted and tried to flee from the task. He did not want to be the bearer of God's word. But, try as he would to escape, Jonah had no choice but to do God's bidding.

"Go to Nineveh," God commanded.

"Who, me?" choked Jonah.

"Yes, you," said God.

"But those people in Nineveh aren't even our kind, they are Gentiles," moaned Jonah.

"Just go," said God.

Jonah promptly took passage on a ship headed the wrong way. That evoked God's anger. A storm blew up, the sailors threw Jonah overboard, a whale swallowed him and spit him out at the gates of Nineveh. In short, Jonah got to Nineveh the hard way. There God demanded that he prophesy to the people. Cursing his fate and despising the people, Jonah reluctantly did what God demanded. And the people, scared, heeded his words and repented. So God spared Nineveh.

The situation into which God put him aroused confusion and anger in Jonah. Who was he? Wasn't he a Hebrew? Then why did God send him to save the people of Nineveh? Didn't everyone know that the people of Nineveh were cruel and bad, and that they were not even Jewish? Why should God expect him to have dealings with faraway people who were different and, therefore, inferior?

Worn out and disgusted, Jonah took refuge from the heat under a shade plant. But the plant suddenly wilted. Jonah even complained to God about that! God answered:

> You cared about the plant, which you did not work for and which you did not grow, which appeared overnight and perished overnight. And should not I care about Nineveh, that great city, in which there are more than a hundred and twenty thousand persons who do not yet know their right hand from their left, and many beasts as well!
>
> Jon. 4:10–11

What kind of nonsense is this for God to send Jonah into the hot sun, far away from home, to help the "inferior and foreign" people of Nineveh? And yet, there was God who, after all, had made a covenant with the Hebrews, getting all softhearted about the poor gentiles of faraway Nineveh—and even their cattle. What did it all mean? What was God trying to prove?

What God was trying to prove was very simple: there is only one human family, and every member of it is God's child. Jonah did not understand what God meant by making the Jews the chosen people. They were not chosen as a master race. As we have learned, they were chosen for special obligation and for special service, to God and to humanity. But while continuing as a distinct group, the Jewish people were also part of the broader family of humanity, and they must never forget that! Jonah forgot; God used him to remind all people that human brotherhood is more important than the separate labels of race, religion, and country that divide human beings from each other.

Then why did God make us different? The rabbis taught us in a Midrash that God made Adam, the first man, out of clay of many different colors so that nobody in the future would ever say, "My race is better than yours." Then why these different races, religions, and nations? Wouldn't there be less hate if we were all one color and had one, universal religion? Why be Jewish? Why be anything other than just human?

Differences make human life full and interesting. Wouldn't life be dull if everybody looked and felt alike? Did you ever go into a neighborhood made up of people of the same background—religious, racial, or economic—living in the same kind of houses? Could anything be duller? It is true that many people still hate people who look and are different from them, but living with and enjoying differences is what gives life its special quality. We can test the truth of this assertion.

PLAY AN IDENTITY GAME

Ask each person to write a sign that says "I AM. . . ." Now make four separate signs for the whole group, reading: "American," "human being," "Jew," "boy/girl." Post each of the four signs on a different wall in the room. Ask each person in the group to choose a sign under which to stand. Anyone who can't decide may sit in the center of the room. Let the discussion leader ask one or two persons from each group to explain their choices. Each group should ask questions of the other groups, challenging their decisions. List the arguments made by each group.

This exercise will reveal that we, too, are in disagreement, and perhaps confused, about our identities. If one person chooses "human being," is that person saying that religious and racial labels interfere with our humanity? Is that true? Does selecting "Jew" indicate that one's ethnic and religious identity is more important than one's humanity? Is the "Jew" less broadminded than the "human being"? Is the "human being" really just running away from accepting who he or she really is? What if an American Jewish family moves to Israel to live? Is the family still American?

The arguments raised by this game revive the ancient, yet still timely, question: "Who am I?" To what group do we belong?

Play another round of the same game. Make individual signs: "When I am older, I would prefer to marry. . . ." Put up these five signs: "an Orthodox Jew," "a New Left radical who has rejected Judaism," "an Israeli career army officer," "a Harvard graduate," "a social worker." Repeat the discussion process. Where did you stand? Why? What values were in conflict, if any? Now, to see an interesting contrast, invite your parents to play the game, either as a group or separately in your individual homes. Did your parents react differently from you? How? Are parents more or less narrowminded than their children? Do they place more or less importance on the survival of the Jewish group?

In playing these games, remember that there is not a right or a wrong answer. There are only your honest feelings and value judgments, what is really important to you, who you really are. Every person—black, Jew, Indian, Mexican, Catholic, Buddhist—goes through life playing the same games of self-identification and defining individual values and beliefs.

A strange experiment was recently conducted in a public school in the small town of Riceville, Iowa. A teacher separated the students into two groups, blue-eyed and brown-eyed. The brown-eyed students were given special privileges; they were told they were better than the blue-eyed group. The "inferior" blue-eyed students could not use the playground, could not get into the lunch line until the brown-eyed ones were through, had to sit in the back of the room, had to wear special collars. What started as a mild game soon became very serious. The "superior" youngsters acted meanly toward their "inferiors." The "inferiors" began to hate their "superiors"; they felt like "dogs on a leash." And, most surprising, the "superiors," who were told they were smarter, did much better in their schoolwork, while the "inferior" youngsters dragged behind. What is the importance of this experiment? How do you think it applies to the racial situation in America?

Did you ever feel fear when you went down into the darkness of a basement at night? That fear, you now know, was foolish. What caused the fear? Did you ever feel fear when you went through a black, Mexican, or Chinese neighborhood? Why were you afraid? Do you remember how you felt your first day in kindergarten? You were probably nervous and afraid. But why?

Some people are afraid of differences.

Many young people are like that. Did you ever belong to a gang? You may know of some gangs in town. What are they for? To keep some people in, but also to keep others out. Sometimes gangs fight each other, even kill one another, over possession of their turf—a park or an empty lot. In our daily lives, we tend to keep out the strange-looking, the handicapped, the "different" person. Isn't that the person we make fun of and pick on? Why do we do it? Because we, too, haven't yet learned to put ourselves in someone else's place. We won't be really human until we do learn, not just to accept, but to enjoy, differences among God's children.

Many people behave the same way when a person of a different race or ethnic group moves into their neighborhood. There have been bloody riots started by people who became terrified at the idea of a black family moving into their all-white neighborhood. Grown men and women have been known to become so upset and frightened when attempts are made to integrate a public school that they attack young children. What could cause such cruelty? Only fear—

fear of change, of someone different, of the unknown and strange. This kind of unreasoning fear on the part of non-Jews once kept Jews out of certain neighborhoods in just about every city in America, and still keeps them out of certain clubs and businesses.

ANTI-SEMITISM AS A FORCE FOR IDENTITY

Recently, a rabbi teaching in a Catholic university told his Catholic students that they could not really understand Jews unless they lived as Jews. As an experiment, the members of the class tried to live as Jews for two weeks. They telephoned their parents and told them they were converting to Judaism and that they were going to marry Jewish partners. They lived among Jews, practiced the Jewish religion and tried to gain every kind of Jewish experience. After two weeks, they began to understand what it meant to live as a Jew in America. Many had been shocked by the anti-Semitism they met in their own parents and loved ones. Do we have to go to such lengths to understand what it means to be a black in America? To be a Puerto Rican? A Roman Catholic? To live on welfare? To be homosexual? To be really human is to feel the hurt and pain that others bear.

Jews have faced anti-Semitism throughout history. We have been persecuted, expelled from countries, humiliated, tortured, and killed merely because we were different. Why, then, should Jews struggle to remain a separate group? Why not just be American, or French, or just human beings?

Aren't we making the same mistake that Jonah made? Doesn't the pride and separateness that every group develops get in the way of our being human beings? Why insist on keeping the "Jewish" label?

We are proud of our history and we believe our people have made important contributions to humankind, and that we have still more to give. We do not respect Jews who turn their backs on their people. We do not respect Jews who change their names and their noses in order to pass as non-Jews. No one can help others unless one respects one's self, accepts one's own roots. People cannot be healthy who deny themselves. There are Jews who are self-haters. But most Jews have a positive feeling about their own Jewishness. A tree with roots can spread its branches very widely. A tree without roots won't stand. People are the same. They, too, need deep, strong roots.

Yet there are some people in our ranks who behave like Jonah. They are so embittered by the persecution Jews have always received that they sneer at non-Jews. They are so angry that Christianity taught hatred of the Jews (as alleged killers of Christ) that they are anti-Christian. Some are anti-black. Some are sexist. All these people commit the same sin as Jonah. It is the sin of separating ourselves from our fellow humans in a spirit of false superiority. It is the sin of generalizing, putting a whole group into one bag. It is the reverse coin of Jew-hatred and it is wrong.

FROM SELF IDENTITY TO IDENTITY WITH OTHERS

The problem of Jonah also applies to the way the Jewish community behaves. There are some Jews who believe that our own Jewish problems are so urgent—Israel must be made secure, Soviet Jews must be helped, anti-Semitism must be fought—that we cannot afford to give some of our energies to causes which affect all people. Therefore, they do not approve when Jewish organizations work for the rights of Chicanos and Indians, the Vietnamese boat people, or anti-poverty programs. These people not only violate the lessons of the book of Jonah; they fly in the face of prophetic Judaism altogether. For the meaning of the prophets is that it is not only our task to keep alive the Jewish people but also, at the same time, to better the world for *all* people. That is our mission, our reason for being.

Being true to one's own faith should not conflict with

respect for other people and other faiths. Do I love Judaism less if I respect Christianity? On the other hand, if I believe my faith is good, do I have a right, even an obligation, to try to convert other people to my faith? Do Christians or Jews for Jesus have a right to try to convert me? Are there lines that can be drawn between proper and improper witnessing?

JEWISH MISSIONIZING

In 1978, Rabbi Alexander M. Schindler, president of the Union of American Hebrew Congregations, proposed that Reform Judaism seek to reach out to converts to Judaism, to the non-Jewish partner of a Jewish spouse, and consider methods to bring the message of Judaism to the unchurched. By "unchurched" he meant those with no formal religious affiliation or faith. Rabbi Schindler also urged Jews to extend a warm welcome to those who had converted to Judaism, as well as to those who, though they may not be formal converts, identify themselves with the Jewish community. His suggestions attracted much attention and stirred some controversy in the Jewish community, particularly his proposal that Jews engage in an active missionary effort. Interestingly, a poll to discover Christian responses to the proposal showed that most Christian leaders did not think Rabbi Schindler's proposals were either inappropriate or threatening to Christianity. What do you think of Rabbi Schindler's proposal? (For a copy of Rabbi Schindler's speech, write to the Union of American Hebrew Congregations.)

In the previous chapter we described the offensive tactics of Jewish-Christians who have aggressively sought to convert Jews. We asked if you felt they were morally correct in their activities. Is it only their tactics which offend, or are they wrong in principle? It is not an easy problem.

Should Jews try to convert non-Jews to Judaism? The Lubavitcher *chasidim* have "Mitzvah Mobiles" that they park in public places, on college campuses, and on the streets of larger communities from which their disciples go, presumably stopping only Jewish people (how can they know?) and trying to persuade them to become Orthodox Jews and to begin practicing some of the rituals of Orthodoxy. Is this a legitimate way to express our mission to the world, as we have come to understand that word from our previous discussion?

There are some Jews who believe that because our numbers are declining, we should mount a more aggressive campaign of introducing Judaism to both Jews and non-Jews. If that is a correct conclusion, how could we do so and, at the same time, avoid the high pressure tactics and arm twisting we Jews so bitterly resent when others do it to us? Do you think such a proselytizing effort could be successful? Do you think such a program would damage Christian-Jewish relations? Are those relations so important that such a risk should be avoided? Would Jews accept converts freely and warmly? Have they in the past? Debate these issues in class.

Judaism has never believed that ours is the only truth. We believe Judaism is good and right—for Jews, and for those who freely choose to become Jews. But we have never presumed that only our way is the right way to God. We have never seen our chosenness as a license for superiority. Judaism respects all other faiths as coequals. We believe that the proper relationship among faiths is to understand each other, to respect each other, and to dialogue with each other. We believe that the best kind of relations among differing groups involves working together toward common goals—to feed the hungry, to combat crime, to control violence, to advance racial justice, to rebuild our cities, to provide jobs, to aid the elderly, and to struggle for peace for all humanity.

IX

Patriotism

THE BUMPER STICKER CONVERSATION

You can learn a lot about people's values from the bumper stickers they put on the backs of their most sacred possessions: their automobiles. You can also learn a lot about your own values from your reactions to those stickers. Take Josh and his friend, Dan.

They'd been up at the lake with Josh's folks. Josh had asked his good friend Dan to spend the weekend with him at the family cottage, and now they were on their way home. Coming down the highway, a Ford sedan whipped by. As it did, Josh caught a glimpse of the bumper sticker pasted on the car's rear end: "America—love it or leave it." An American flag was in the middle of the red, white, and blue background. Dan had seen it, too. The two boys looked at each other and immediately resumed the argument they had been having all weekend at the lake. "See," said Josh, "that's what I mean. Guys like that think it's so simple. Either you're a fanatic on everything that America does, supporting it all the way, or you're a traitor. If you don't like it here, go somewhere else. They make me sick."

Josh and Dan had gotten into the argument because Josh's older brother, Pete, had left the United States in 1968 after being drafted into the army. He fled rather than fight in the Vietnam War. He had escaped to live in Canada and had never come back for fear of being arrested as a deserter.

Dan reacted. "I know you miss your brother, but what did you expect? After all, Pete is a deserter. He ran out on his country." That did it, and the argument that began then had lasted all weekend.

As the car with the bumper sticker disappeared down the road, Josh picked up the discussion again. "Guys like that think they've got some kind of a lock on patriotism and, what's worse, they try to make guys like Pete look like traitors. They're trying to tell us that if you don't believe in 'my country right or wrong' you're unpatriotic or disloyal. Why, if they were really right, we'd still be in Vietnam, and we'd still have Nixon in the White House, and the whole Watergate bit would still be buried. And what a lousy price Pete's paying for it all. He's still in Canada, an exile who can't come home."

"Well, I'm sorry, but why should he be able to? He ran away from his patriotic duty, didn't he?" asked Dan.

"The heck he did," Josh yelled. "He did what he felt was right. Who says it's better to kill a bunch of Vietnamese 12,000 miles away than it is to say I can't in good conscience kill anyone, especially in a war I believe is stupid?"

"But it was the law, Josh," Dan argued. "You can't go around breaking the law every time you disagree with it. It's unpatriotic. Just imagine what would happen if everyone did that?"

The two boys argued all the way back to the city. Neither really convinced the other. Truthfully, there was a lot of merit in each of their arguments. The Vietnam War and the scandal of Watergate left a lot of Americans torn about the meaning of patriotism. This has become a vexing problem for millions of Americans. But the meaning of patriotism is a problem for all nations. In South Africa, millions of blacks are beginning to rise up in militant protest against the racist laws of a minority of whites. This conflict over what is truly patriotic, and over the question of whether people have the right to challenge the government in order to achieve justice, continues to be a great problem in American life, too, as it has been in all lands at all times.

What this leads to is the question: *Does the end justify the means?* In other words, if your goal is a good one, is any way you choose to reach that goal acceptable? Or must the means be as good as the goal? Let us cite a few examples to clarify the problem. Let us say that black people in a certain community are subjected to cruel and unfair treatment. They live in a slum; their average rate of unemployment is about 20 percent (and, for young men, it goes as high as 40 percent); the rents they are forced to pay for decaying and rat-infested tenements are high; merchandise sold to them in the stores is frequently inferior, and the prices are exorbitant. Police officers patrolling the black neighborhood have often been brutal to the local people and, even more often, rude and contemptuous. Finally, an incident triggers the anger of the residents. A riot breaks out. The stores, which had overcharged them, are looted. Some of the worst tenements are firebombed. A black youth leader, in an interview on television, cries: "We are not rioting; we are rebelling against inhuman conditions! We will not be treated like animals any longer! We are demanding justice!"

No fair-minded person can deny the ugly conditions under which these people were forced to live. The question then becomes: Is violence a proper means through which to work for justice? The black person caught up in this situation might laugh at the question, and might say, "We tried to get justice by lawful and legal means and nothing happened. Nobody knew we were alive until we rattled our cages! What choice did we have?" On the other hand, even the best goals in the world can be soiled by bad methods of trying to achieve them. Is that the case in this situation? Why or why not? Which course is patriotic?

What follows is a true story that took place during World War II. A short (ten-minute) movie has been made about this incident. It is called *Joseph Shultz.* *

* This film may be ordered for group viewing through the Jewish Media Service, 15 E. 26th Street, New York, N.Y. 10010, and might be shown in conjunction with this discussion.

Joseph Shultz was an ordinary soldier in the German army during World War II. Like most of the millions of men and women who were drafted into that nation's military service, Shultz allowed himself to be drafted as part of his patriotic duty. He probably wasn't a Nazi. Many German soldiers were not. We don't know whether he thought Hitler's desire to conquer the world was morally right or wrong. All we can assume is that he, like hundreds of thousands of Germans during this time, was afraid that he would be either imprisoned or shot as a traitor if he didn't go into the army. Maybe Shultz felt that to refuse to put on a uniform at a time when Germany was involved in a world war was to shirk his duty as a loyal citizen of his nation.

After his basic training, Joseph Shultz was sent to the front, where he did what he was ordered to do. As his unit moved from town to town, occupying and securing the countryside, he moved with them, killing enemy soldiers, blowing up targets, both military and civilian, and in general trying to keep from being killed.

One day his commanding officer ordered his platoon to march to the outskirts of a town and to form into a firing squad. In front of him a group of twenty local civilians, men and women, stood blindfolded in front of a huge haystack. Shultz and his platoon were ordered to line up, raise their rifles, aim, and, at the command, fire. All the soldiers dutifully began to follow the orders. All except Shultz. When ordered to raise his rifle, he froze at attention. The lieutenant ordered him specifically: "Put your rifle on your shoulder, Shultz." Shultz refused. Instead, slowly, methodically, very carefully, he put his gun down in front of him, took off his cartridge belt—the clasp of which had engraved on it *Gott mit uns,* "God is with us"—removed his army jacket, which he neatly folded and placed on top of his rifle, then his dog tags which he placed on top of his jacket. Finally, he took off his helmet and placed that on top of the rest, marched to the haystack, and joined the group of civilians, where he took the hands of those on either side of him, turned, and faced the group of soldiers who until that moment had been his comrades in arms. He stood silently, waiting.

For a minute, so did his commanding officer. He glared at Shultz, unbelieving. Then he turned to the firing squad, all of whom were standing with their guns on their shoulders, aimed at the group, their fingers on the triggers. "Fire!" he commanded. The dozen rifles shot like one, and the group at the haystack fell instantly—all but one. Private Joseph Shultz remained standing. Not one of his buddies had aimed at him. The lieutenant was beside himself with rage and frustration. He screamed at his men: "Fire! Fire! Fire!" Private Shultz crumpled against the body of one of the civilians whose hand he had been holding only a minute before. The bullets tore a gaping hole in Shultz. He was dead. The platoon shouldered their weapons and, at the command of their officer in charge, marched from the field. A German officer who witnessed the incident took snapshots of the entire episode. They were found later by the Allies.

Private Joseph Shultz was shot as a traitor. Was he a traitor? Did patriotism demand that he kill innocent civilians in cold blood? If Shultz failed to obey the order of his commanding officer, was he obeying some higher authority? To whom was Shultz listening? German soldiers wore the phrase "God is with us" on their belt buckles. Was God with Shultz, or with his fellow soldiers who shot him? Was God with the innocent civilians facing slaughter? Was God with anyone at all in that bloody field on that horrible day? What would happen to an army if, during a war (or peacetime), individual soldiers took it upon themselves to make moral judgments on the orders given them by their superiors? Probably the lieutenant was himself obeying an order given him by someone higher in the chain of command. Was he more patriotic than the private? What is patriotism, and are there limits to it, especially if the demands a nation makes on its citizens run counter to their deepest ideas of right and wrong?

THE JEWS IN PALESTINE

Jews have faced the same terrible problem of means and ends many times. Let us cite a painful example. Right after World War II, the Jews of Palestine worked desperately to save their fellow Jews who were still alive in Europe after Hitler had killed six million of their brothers and sisters. This was before the State of Israel was established in 1948. Palestine was then under the control of the British, and the Jews were prohibited from bringing in displaced persons. It was illegal for Jews to bring refugee ships into Haifa. The goal of the Jewish community of Palestine was twofold: to save the refugees from Hitler by bringing them to Palestine, and to force the British to permit the Jews to establish their own state as the British had once promised in the Balfour Declaration. What means should (or could) be used to accomplish these goals?

The Jews decided to defy the British law, which they declared to be inhuman. And so, a number of battered old ships were bought to carry Jews to Israel. Two of them were the *Exodus* and *Altalena.* They set sail from Europe with thousands of pitiful survivors of the concentration camps trying desperately to run the British blockade of the Mediterranean. Given their goal, did the Jews have the right to follow this illegal means?

A small minority of the Jews in Palestine decided that they could not achieve their goals without the use of force. And so, when the British captured and hanged Jewish underground leaders in Palestine, the members of the *Irgun* (and the Stern Gang), Jewish extremists, captured and hanged British soldiers in reprisal. Most Jews in Palestine, and the great majority of Jews throughout the world, were horrified by the bloody actions of these extremists. The same old questions: Did the end justify the means? Can you reach a decent goal with indecent means?

In 1977, Menachem Begin was elected Prime Minister of Israel. The first reaction throughout the world, including

the Jewish world, was shock and shame. For Begin had been
a leader of the Irgun in the days before Israel was created.
In the eyes of the world he had been a terrorist, but to Jews
he was a Jewish fighter for liberation. Some thought it a
disgrace that the Jewish state should be headed by a person
of violence. Would you agree or disagree? In making a judgment, you must bear in mind that the Jewish terrorists, unlike the current P.L.O. terrorists, never deliberately tried to
hurt civilians. They did not proclaim the goal of genocide
against any people. Even so, they were condemned by most
Jews in Palestine and throughout the world. Moreover, Mr.
Begin joined the government when Israel was created and
loyally served in the opposition party until he was elected
by the free choice of democratic Israel.

The Choice of Conscience

This haunting problem of conscience is the subject of a
book entitled *Dawn,* written by Elie Wiesel, who was himself a survivor of Hitler's concentration camps. In *Dawn,* a
young Jew somehow escapes death in one of Hitler's
camps; most of his family is wiped out. He manages to get
to Palestine on an illegal ship. There he becomes a member of the underground Irgun. One night his superiors
order him to kill a British soldier as a reprisal against the
execution of a Jewish underground fighter by the British.
The young Jew is told that he must execute the prisoner at
dawn. All night long the torments of conscience pound at
the young man. He is torn between what he thinks Jewish
ideals are and what he thinks Jews must do in that desperate hour to survive in the world. The debate rages all night
in his head. One side says to him:

> . . . We have no other choice. For generations we have
> waited to be better, more pure in heart than those who
> persecuted us. You've all seen the result: Hitler and the

extermination camps in Germany. We'd had enough of trying to be more just than those who claim to speak in the name of justice . . . if ever it's a question of killing off Jews, everyone is silent; there are twenty centuries of history to prove it . . . The Commandment, thou shalt not murder, was given from the summit of one of the mountains here in Palestine and we were the only ones to obey it. But that's all over. We must be like everyone else.

But, whispering like a shadow in his mind, comes the argument from the opposite side: ". . . Where is God to be found? In suffering or in rebellion? When is a man most truly a man? When he submits or when he refuses? Where does suffering lead him? To purification or to bestiality?"

We won't tell you what he finally decided. Read the book to find out. But the debate between Jewish ideals and practical necessity goes on in each of us all the time. So does the endless question of the relation between ends and means, between conscience and the demand of society for patriotic obedience.

Our ancestors asked the same kinds of questions in the time of the prophets. The patriotism of the prophets was severely challenged. What was the patriotism of the prophets?

PROPHETIC DISSENT

They were dissenters. They believed that anyone who is silent in the face of evil is an accomplice to the evil. They did not believe, as so many people do, that God was always on their side. They believed that God was on the side of right and the purpose of prophecy was to induce the people to get on God's (the right) side. To the prophets, the measure of the country was its moral character, not its wealth, prestige or power. Israel was chosen by God to be "a blessing" and a "light unto the nations." Therefore, if Israel acted without mercy or justice, it must be condemned and called back to its rightful place.

The life of Jeremiah shows in most dramatic form the differing ideas people had about patriotism.

Jeremiah was summoned by God as a young lad. God told him he must prophesy against the priests of the Temple, the rulers of the land, and the people themselves—"against the whole land." It would be rough; Jeremiah would be scorned and he would suffer terribly. Jeremiah pleaded that he was too young; God insisted. Jeremiah reluctantly became a prophet, speaking the words of God, even when he faced the threat of death for treason.

> I thought, "I will not mention Him,
> No more will I speak in His name"—
> But [His word] was like a raging fire in my heart,
> Shut up in my bones;
> I could not hold it in, I was helpless.
>
> Jer. 20:9

These words of Jeremiah describe the torment of conscience which sensitive people of all generations have felt.

Jeremiah was a stormy figure. In the Temple he castigated the priests and rich worshippers for their empty rituals. God wants justice, not hollow gestures, he charged. He went on trial for his life and, once freed, refused to be silent. He accused King Jehoiakim, a puppet of the Egyptians who ruled Judah at that time, of having betrayed his God and his faith. Fearlessly, Jeremiah predicted that the vile king would die, unlamented, and that he would "be buried with the burial of an ass." One day, Jeremiah sent Baruch, his scribe, to read the scroll of Jeremiah's words to the king. The king listened coldly to the warning of doom if he, and the people, did not repent. As each part of the scroll was read, the king cut it with a knife and threw it into the fire. He then ordered the arrest of both Baruch and Jeremiah.

Undaunted, Jeremiah dictated the entire scroll from

memory to Baruch all over again, adding some new sections for good measure. Censorship did not frighten him; it made him bolder. Then, as Jeremiah had predicted, Babylonia conquered Judea and 8,000 Judeans were taken away in sorrow in the beginning of the Babylonian exile. The new king of Judea decided to revolt against the Babylonians. Jeremiah was terrified. He knew the revolt would fail, and the Jewish people would be destroyed. He begged the king to surrender to Babylonia and wait for better times and ultimate return to Judah. While the war fever coursed through the people, Jeremiah pleaded with them not to resist but to surrender, to submit to exile.

Naturally, he was thrown into prison. Some of the palace aides insisted he be put to death as a traitor, particularly when they learned Jeremiah had written a letter to the Jews already exiled to Babylonia, urging them to forget all about an early return to Zion. The aging prophet was beaten and hurled into a hellish dungeon. As the siege of Judah continued, the king of Judah, in desperation, called Jeremiah and asked him: "Is there any word from the Lord?" Jeremiah could have freed himself by saying what the king wanted to hear. Instead, he prophesied: "This city shall be delivered into the hands of the king of Babylon's army" (Jer. 38:3). He begged the king, once more, to surrender and save the people. The king refused and, in his frustration, he ordered that the prophet be left to die of starvation in a cistern. "They let Jeremiah down by ropes. There was no water in the pit, only mud, and Jeremiah sank into the mud" (Jer. 38:6).

Jeremiah was saved from the pit, but Judah could not be saved from its grim fate. On the ninth day of the Hebrew month of *Av* in the year 586 B.C.E., Nebuchadnezzar's army, with their battering rams, smashed through the walls of Jerusalem. That date is still mourned by Jewish people throughout the world every year, as *Tishah Be'av*.

Was Jeremiah a traitor? Or was he a patriot? What would he say if he were alive today? How would he be received? Are there people alive today who have within them the fire of conscience which made Jeremiah so unforgettable and lonely a figure? Must a prophet be resigned to a sad and solitary life? What good did Jeremiah's suffering really do? One thing is clear. His words have echoed through time, down to the present, and his truth continues to shake humanity. The lonely youth from Anathoth has proved to be immortal. Through him, God has spoken to all ages—and speaks still to ours, warning us to "mend our ways."

Jeremiah came as a radical, "to uproot and to pull down, to destroy and to overthrow" (Jer. 1:10) in order to inspire the people "to build and to plant" (Jer. 1:10). He was a rebel with a cause. The cause is still here and, thank God, there are still rebels who place their lives on the line to cry out for justice, for mercy, and for peace.

Based on the lessons of the prophets, we have a right to be skeptical of those self-proclaimed patriots who claim to be acting in behalf of God and country. In America, even the hooded moguls of the K.K.K. always claim they speak for God and country. What God wants may or may not be the same as what any country wants. The great American writer, Mark Twain, was struck by the fact that in the Spanish-American War, both the Americans and the Spaniards believed that God was on their side. The following is Twain's mocking prayer:*

> O Lord our Father, our young patriots,
> idols of our hearts, go forth to battle—
> be Thou near them! With them, in spirit,
> we also go forth from the sweet peace
> of our beloved firesides to smite the foe.
> O Lord our God, help us to tear their soldiers
> to bloody shreds with our shells;
> help us to cover their smiling fields
> with the pale forms of their patriot dead;

* *The War Prayer* (St. Crispin Press Book, co-publisher, Harper & Row, 1968).

help us to drown the thunder of the guns
with the shrieks of their wounded,
writhing in pain;
help us to lay waste their humble homes
with a hurricane of fire;
help us to wring the hearts
of their unoffending widows
with unavailing grief;
help us to turn them out roofless
with their children to wander unfriended
the wastes of their desolated land
in rags and hunger and thirst,
sports of the sun, flames of summer
and the icy winds of winter,
broken in spirit, worn with travail,
imploring Thee for the refuge of the grave
and denied it—
for our sakes who adore Thee, Lord,
blast their hopes, blight their lives,
protract their bitter pilgrimage,
make heavy their steps,
water their way with their tears,
stain the white snow with the blood
of their wounded feet!
We ask it, in the spirit of love,
of Him Who is the Source of Love,
and Who is the ever-faithful refuge and friend
of all that are sore beset and seek His aid
with humble and contrite hearts.
Amen.

What is Mark Twain trying to tell us in this prayer? Do you
agree or not? We Jews in recent times have seen the disaster
which comes from blind "my country, right or wrong" patriotism. When Adolf Hitler took over Germany, he set out on
the bloodiest mission in the history of the world. One part
of the program was the slaughter of all the Jews. He almost
succeeded; he killed one of every three Jews then living in
the world. Many "good Germans" knew that Hitler was
carrying out this savage butchery, but they felt it their patriotic duty to keep silent, to support their government, right

or wrong. Was this proper patriotism? After the war, the
Allies held an international tribunal and sentenced to death
many of the Nazis who murdered innocent people because
they were ordered to. The tribunal, called the Nuremberg
Trials, declared the principle that every person is responsible to his or her own conscience and that the claims of
conscience, or God, are higher than that of obedience to
one's own government.

In Modern America

The Vietnam War sharpened the conflicts about patriotism
in the United States. Millions of Americans decided that, in
conscience, they could not participate in a war that went
against their ideas of right and wrong. Some refused to pay
taxes which would be used to continue the war. Some young
men became conscientious objectors because they refused
to kill. Some, like Pete in our story, fled their country rather
than serve in a war they felt was wrong. Some soldiers re-
quested an honorable release from the armed forces because of their convictions. A few Americans actively disrupted the draft to protest the war; a group of Catholic
priests and lay people were arrested for breaking into a draft
board in Baltimore to pour animal blood on the files to dram-
atize their profound revolt against the war. Which of these
acts were patriotic? Which were unpatriotic? Which of these
should be protected by the law? Which, in your opinion,
should be punished? What would you do if you had been a
draft-age male like Pete and felt bound in conscience to
oppose the war? What would prophets, like Jeremiah, have
said and done if they were alive at that time?
    There is an organization of radical and militant Jews
called the Jewish Defense League. This group has sometimes broken laws in demonstrating for Soviet Jewry. Did
they have a right to do this? Did these violent acts help to
make things better or not? Dissent, disagreeing, is every

American's right. But violent dissent is illegal. Is it always wrong? Can you give other examples? Is violent dissent ever right? Was the Boston Tea Party legal?

One can easily see the many things that are wrong in America in our age, too—racial injustice, drugs, pollution, war, slums, poverty, corruption. But do we have the right to break a law just because we don't approve of it? Our drug laws are generally felt to be unwise and ineffective. A few states still punish users of marijuana in the same way that they treat users of hard drugs like heroin. Obviously these laws have not prevented a dread epidemic of drugs from sweeping through every community and destroying millions of lives. But does one who regards our drug laws as "stupid" have the moral right to ignore the law because he or she doesn't approve of it?

When law breaks down, people consume each other. A responsible person works for change and protests evil, but at the same time seeks to preserve the system of law without which the society will be reduced to a jungle-like existence. Imagine if every person ignored traffic laws. Would that be just? How much worse it would be if everyone ignored the just demands of the law which, in a free society, apply to everyone equally. No society can succeed if everyone does what is right in their own eyes and shows contempt for the law. Certainly the prophets did not urge a society of lawlessness.

PROPHETIC PATRIOTS

We've already talked about Jeremiah, but let's take a look at what some of the other prophets had to say about patriotism. It would not be difficult to accuse some of them also of being unpatriotic.

Amos, for example, was thrown out of the town of Bethel on the charge of conspiracy against the king. Amos was so disgusted by the people's corrupt and immoral be-

havior that he prophesied that God would rise up to destroy
King Jeroboam and his entire household. He warned that in
the approaching day of doom, all the sanctuaries and altars
would be destroyed. In some of the most vivid and powerful
language to be found in any of the prophetic writings, Amos
gives us a clear picture of the condition in northern Israel
at this time. The rich were getting richer by oppressing the
poor. A few lived in luxury, while the majority lived in total
poverty and despair.

> Thus said the Lord:
> For three transgressions of Israel,
> For four, I will not revoke it:
> Because they have sold for silver
> Those whose cause was just,
> And the needy for a pair of sandals.
>
> Amos 2:6

The poor, forced to borrow at impossibly high rates, found
themselves driven more deeply into debt, until they sold
themselves and their children into slavery. The wealthy felt
no pity. To the contrary:

> [Ah,] you who trample the heads of the poor
> Into the dust of the ground,
> And make the humble walk a twisted course!
> Father and son go to the same girl,
> And thereby profane My holy name.
>
> Amos 2:7

They would even take the clothes off the backs of the poor
as security for a loan, and "They recline by every altar on
garments taken in pledge" (Amos 2:8). Such behavior was a
clear violation of the ethical commands given earlier to the
people by Moses:

> If, however, there is a needy person among you, one of
> your kinsmen in any of your settlements in the land that

the Lord your God is giving you, do not harden your heart and shut your hand against your needy kinsman. Rather, you must open your hand and lend him sufficient for whatever he needs.

Deut. 15:7–8

Moreover, this behavior violated the rules under which loans should be made:

If you lend money to My people, to the poor who is in your power, do not act toward him as a creditor: exact no interest from him.

Ex. 22:24

It also disregarded the rules governing pledges and security:

If you take your neighbor's garment in pledge, you must return it to him before the sun sets; it is his only clothing, the sole covering for his skin. In what else shall he sleep? Therefore, if he cries out to Me, I will pay heed, for I am compassionate.

Ex. 22:25–26

But these were not Israel's only sins, according to Amos:

. . . you have turned justice into poison weed
And the fruit of righteousness to wormwood.

Amos 6:12

They cared only for money, saying:

If only the new moon were over, so that we could sell grain; the sabbath, so that we could offer wheat for sale.

Amos 8:5

They cheated their customers

> ... using an ephah that is too small, and a shekel that is too
> big, tilting a dishonest scale, and selling grain refuse as
> grain! We will buy the poor for silver, the needy for a pair
> of sandals.
>
> Amos 8:5–6

And while the majority of the people suffered in poverty,
the rich and privileged class lay

> ... on ivory beds,
> Lolling on their couches,
> Feasting on lambs from the flock
> And on calves from the stalls.
> ... They drink [straight] from the wine bowls
> And anoint themselves with the choicest oils—
> But they are not concerned about the ruin of Joseph.
>
> Amos 6:4,6

Amos, seeing all this, could not restrain himself. He lashed
out at the king and his priests who tolerated such injustice.
He denounced them with scathing sarcasm.

> Come to Bethel and transgress;
> To Gilgal and transgress even more:
> Present your sacrifices the next morning
> And your tithes on the third day;
> And burn a thank offering of leavened bread;
> And proclaim freewill offerings loudly.
> For you love that sort of thing, O Israelites.
>
> Amos 4:4–5

It would do no good even if they observed the rituals. Amos
prophesied:

> I loathe, I spurn your festivals,
> I am not appeased by your solemn assemblies.
> If you offer Me burnt offerings—or your meal offerings—

> I will not accept them;
> I will pay no heed
> To your gifts of fatlings.
>
> Amos 5:21–22

This is not what God desires; rather, God demands that

> . . . justice well up like water,
> Righteousness like an unfailing stream.
>
> Amos 5:24

Because that is absent, the kingdom will be destroyed.

> A time is coming—declares my Lord God—when I will send a famine upon the land: not a hunger for bread or a thirst for water, but for hearing the words of the Lord. Men shall wander from sea to sea and from north to east to seek the word of the Lord, but they shall not find it.
>
> Amos 8:11–12

Little wonder that the priest and king wanted Amos thrown out.

> . . . Amos is conspiring against you within the House of Israel. The country cannot endure the things he is saying.
>
> Amos 7:10

And Amos was banished.

> . . . Seer, off with you to the land of Judah! Earn your living there, and do your prophesying there. But don't ever prophesy again at Bethel; for it is a king's sanctuary and a royal palace.
>
> Amos 7:12–13

"Our country, love it or leave it!"

Of course, Amos proved to be right. Within 30 years, the northern kingdom of Israel was destroyed by the Assyrians and no one knows what happened to the people. Today they are known only as the Ten Lost Tribes.

During World War II, hundreds of thousands of Japanese-Americans living on the West Coast were rounded up by the United States government and, without any explanation or trial, were shipped to detention camps in Arizona and New Mexico where they lived behind barbed wire for the entire duration of the war. Most of those so detained were American citizens, and many had children who fought against the Nazis and the Japanese in the American armed forces. Second only to what we did to our native American Indians, this was probably the worst injustice our government ever committed against a group of its citizens. During the war, practically no one protested what was done to the Nisei, as they were called. They were afraid to. They were afraid of being called traitors. Was that patriotism or cowardice? What would the prophets have said?

Were the prophets unpatriotic? They didn't think so. On the contrary, they believed they were acting within a well-established tradition of criticism. They knew the history of Nathan's criticism of David, of Elijah's denunciation of Ahab; and they believed they were acting in that tradition. If they were critical of their country's government, it was not because they wanted to see it destroyed but, on the contrary, because they wished to see it *live*. They believed that, because of its small size, its strategic geographical location, being the center of a natural land bridge between Egypt, Asia Minor, and routes to the north and west, it could not afford to make political alliances (usually with Egypt) to ward off attacks from other more powerful nations and empires. Most of the prophets condemned these kinds of efforts. (See Hosea 5:13, 7:11–12.)

THE MEANING OF PATRIOTISM

The prophets were what we would call today political isola-
tionists. Would people listen to them today? Probably not.
Were they right in their time? Yes, but for reasons other
than practical political considerations. They knew that political alliances usually brought religious influences as well.
They feared that the pure worship of God would be ruined
by such alliances, which would bring the worship of foreign
gods into Palestine. The kind of political and military pacts
that the kingdoms of Israel and Judah entered into suggested a distrust of God. For the prophets, only trust in God
could eventually save the Jewish people (Isa. 30:15). To the
prophets, only God was able to overrule human efforts. God
could and would use foreign powers to punish Israel for its
violation of the ethical commandments, but God could also
destroy foreign nations if they became too proud.

But the prophets were not pacifists. They did not object
to the use of force as such, only to a futile reliance upon
military power to solve problems caused by the far more
serious problem of violating God's justice (Isa. 31:1–3;
22:8–11).

Most interesting was Isaiah's belief that war corrupts
the moral standards of a people. He knew that there was a
war psychology which tends to justify behavior that is otherwise unjustifiable.

The patriotism of the prophets was not negative. They
had very definite positive goals in mind. They wanted the
people and their leaders to be true to God and to the covenant. They wanted them to be a people who were just and
righteous in the sight of God. In order to be such a people,
said the prophets, they must realize that the capacity to do
evil was to be found within themselves as well as within their
enemies. The prophets challenged the people to see that
their difficulties and their tragedies were usually the result
of their own failures, and not what their enemies did to
them. The people suffered from false leadership by rulers

who tried to do their own will, rather than the will of God. They were guilty of taking advantage of the poor. They suffered from false national pride and from a narrowness of vision which caused them to believe that God was theirs only and not a God of all peoples. The greatness of the Hebrew people could never be in military or commercial power, but only in moral and spiritual power. Were the prophets right? All the nations who surrounded Israel and who dominated her militarily, commercially, even culturally, no longer exist. They are fossilized, found only in the museums of the world. But the Jewish people lives, "not by might, nor by power, but by my spirit—said the Lord of Hosts" (Zech. 4:6). On the other hand, how long would modern Israel survive without military power?

The prophetic definition of patriotism does not tell us that one's state is always right and that one must be ready to defend its every action. It rejects the idea of "my country, right or wrong." It rejects the idea that in social and political crisis, an individual must remain silent. On the contrary, narrow nationalistic patriotism was seen as totally wrong. Real patriotism is to see the nation in the context of the larger world and in the framework of what is ultimately morally and spiritually just. Real patriotism seeks for the total welfare of the people of one's own country, not merely the success of a few or of a specific group. Moreover, the good of those who live in other states must be sought. False patriotism says, "My country right or wrong." Genuine patriotism—the kind the prophets expressed in their words and their lives—says, "My country, when right to be upheld, when wrong to be made right."

Love for one's country, and for one's people, is a good and healthy feeling. But to look down on other peoples as if they are lesser breeds of humanity is not patriotism, it is racism. Also, one should love one's country, but should not do so blindly. Just as we criticize members of our own family whom we love, so we should criticize what is wrong in our own country. Love of country, however, should never take precedence over love of God. If the demands of God and country are ever in conflict, God must come first. In this sense, "My country, right or wrong" is paganism and idolatry because the first Commandment says, "You shall have no other gods beside Me." Those gods even include country. For God is not the private toy of China, Russia, the United States, Israel, or any other nation. God is the Sovereign of all the world!

X

Peace

YOU may have heard of a musical called *Shenandoah*, which appeared on Broadway (and was also made into a movie). It was about a family who lived in the Shenandoah Valley of Virginia during the Civil War. The father refused to join the Confederate cause or to let his six sons fight in the war. He felt that war was stupid and wrong, and so he decided to remain neutral—above the battle, tending his own farm.

His sons felt guilty about sitting out the war and argued with their father about it. One of them, James, 26 years old, said: "I know how you feel about this war, Pa. . . . And I guess we all feel more or less the same way, but I don't know how we can just sit here and ignore it any longer. You say it's no business of ours and not our fight. Well, we're Virginians."

Charlie (the father) answers: "I'm an American."

James: "Yes, but we're still Virginians, and . . . and I believe that what concerns Virginia concerns us. . . ."

Charlie: "As far as I can see, James, this farm is exactly the way it's always been, and this farm and the people at this table are the only concerns I have in this world. . . . If those fools want to slaughter one another, that's their business, but it's got nothing to do with us. Not one damn thing has it got to do with us."

He then sings the following song:

Stand and show your colors
Let's all go to war.
The Lord will surely bless us
I've heard it all before.

I've heard it all a hundred times
I've heard it all before.
They always got a holy cause
To march you off to war.

Tyranny or justice,
Anarchy or law,
We must defend our honor
I've heard it all before.
I've heard it all a hundred times,
I've heard it all before.
They always got a holy cause
That's what the dying's for.

Someone writes a slogan
Raises up a flag—
Someone finds an enemy to blame
The trumpet sounds the call to arms
To leave the cities and the farms
And always—
The ending is the same
The same
The same
The same.

The dream has turned to ashes
The wheat has turned to straw
And someone asks the questions
What was the dyin' for?
The living can't remember
The dead no longer care.
But next time it won't happen
Upon my soul, I swear.

I've heard it all a hundred times,
I've heard it all before.
Don't tell me "it's different now"
I've heard it all—I've heard it all
I've heard it all before.

And so the Andersons stay out of the war. When a recruiting patrol comes to the farm to try to take his sons, Charlie Anderson says to the lieutenant: "I want you to give me one good reason why I should send my family, that took me a lifetime to raise, down that road like damn fools to do somebody else's fighting."

Johnson, the lieutenant, replies: "Virginia needs all her sons, Mr. Anderson."

Charlie: "That may be, but these are my sons. They don't belong to the state. When they were babies, I never saw the state coming around with a spare tit. We've never asked anything of the state and never expected anything. We do our own living, and thanks to no man for the right."

But Charlie Anderson can't keep the war from touching his family. His youngest son is kidnapped by Union troops, another son and daughter-in-law are killed by marauders, and a third son is accidentally shot to death by a Confederate patrol.

Toward the end of the play, he sorrowfully reflects: "There's nothing much I can tell you about this war. It . . . it's like all wars, I suppose—the undertakers are winning it." And then, in a final song, he reflects on a profound truth:

> The dream has turned to ashes
> The wheat has turned to straw
> And someone asks the question
> What was the dying for?
> The graves are filled with answers
> Each one just and true
> For all men finally reason
> What else could I do?
>
> I heard the drums, the distant guns
> I tried to turn away
> But in the end, the price of peace
> Was more than I could pay.
> I have no shame, I lay no blame
> At someone else's door
> And so the seeds of hate are sown

That blow from war to war
What for, O Lord, what for?

In many ways, Charlie Anderson was right—too right. War is a dreadful, terrible evil, the ultimate inhuman experience. As we look back on the conditions that sparked the Civil War in this country, it is probable that, had people of good will persisted, they could have resolved the issues between the North and the South without resorting to war.

War is humankind's most continuous activity. Any day, somewhere in the world, people murder one another legally. Sometimes the cause for this is the need a nation feels for more living space; sometimes it is the desire for more wealth. Sometimes nations fight to defend themselves against invasion or domination by another country. Sometimes a community of people fight either to force their ideas on another group or to resist somebody else's ideas. Sometimes it is no more and no less a notion than national pride that drives a nation to war. The causes of wars are as complex as they are endless.

Nevertheless, neither the terrible costs of war in life and property nor its irrationality have ever stopped people from engaging in it. Despite the fact that most people would agree that war creates more problems of human misery, economic poverty, and social chaos than it solves, nations continue to make war. It seems that many people still believe it is easier to resolve differences by fighting than by talking and compromise. You have probably seen that situation among your own friends and classmates. And you have probably seen how hard it is to stay out of a fight once it has begun or once you have been challenged. Those who refuse to fight are usually called "yellow" or cowards. They are often humiliated and sometimes forced to run away to avoid being dragged in.

But is fighting ever justifiable? What about World War II and Hitler's drive to conquer the world, imposing on it

rule by a German "master race"? Was it wrong for the allies
to resist Hitler's attempt to destroy the world, beginning
with the destruction of 6,000,000 Jews? What about Israel's
many wars with the Arab nations? What does Judaism say
about war? Is war sometimes right? Under what circumstances?

No one can deny that the history of the Jewish people
is filled with examples of war. Indeed, the biblical record
before the prophets, as well as some of the teachings of the
prophets themselves, encouraged the early Hebrews to engage in war in order to preserve their nation and their way
of life. Yet Judaism deplored war and urged its people first
and foremost to seek peace. As we shall see, the justification
for going to war was carefully spelled out, as were the rules
by which wars could be fought.

The prophets of Israel were both realists and idealists.
On one hand, they dreamed of the time when people would
"beat their swords into plowshares and their spears into
pruning hooks, [when] nation shall not take up sword against
nation; they shall never again know war. But every man
shall sit under his grapevine or fig tree with no one to disturb
him" (Mic. 4:3–4; also Isa. 2:4).

The prophets sincerely wanted to see a peaceful world.
They wanted Israel to be a leader in the pursuit of peace. To
"seek peace and pursue it," a phrase found in Ps. 34:15,
became a watchword of the faith of Israel.

The most glorious visions of the prophets are devoted
to the time when the lion and the lamb shall lie down together.

> The wolf shall dwell with the lamb,
> The leopard lie down with the kid;
> The calf, the beast of prey, and the fatling together,
> With a little boy to herd them.
> The cow and the bear shall graze,
> Their young shall lie down together;
> And the lion, like the ox, shall eat straw.
> A babe shall play

Over a viper's hole,
And an infant pass his hand
Over an adder's den.
In all of My sacred mount
Nothing evil or vile shall be done;
For the land shall be filled with devotion to the Lord
As water covers the sea.

Isa. 11:6–9

Peace was seen by the prophets as an attainable goal to be realized as people accepted and lived under the discipline of what the prophets considered the law of God.

At the same time, they realized that no nation should be expected to commit suicide by turning the other cheek against an aggressor. When the Jewish people were threatened with national destruction, the prophets would reverse the image of the plowshares described earlier. Then the defense of the country became a duty from which the nation could not escape.

Proclaim this among the nations:
Prepare for battle!
Arouse the warriors,
Let all the fighters come and draw near!
Beat your plowshares into swords,
And your pruning hooks into spears.
Let even the weakling say, "I am strong."
Rouse yourselves and come,
All you nations;
Come together
From round about.
There bring down
Your warriors, O Lord!

Joel 4:9–11

Ancient peoples had no conception of international law or international justice. Each nation saw itself as supreme, standing against every other nation. Each had its own god to protect it from its enemies and the calamities of nature. Before Israel, no nation and no people thought of God as

One, supreme over all other gods and nations, knowing no
favorites. It was the prophet Amos who expanded the concept, portraying the One God as a universal Lord, source of
one law for all humanity, with one international justice for
all. God, said the prophet Amos, is not only the God of Israel,
but also the God of all other nations:

> To Me, O Israelites, you are
> Just like Ethiopians
> > —declares the Lord.

> True, I brought Israel up
> From the land of Egypt,
> But also the Philistines from Caphtor
> And the Arameans from Kir.
> > Amos 9:7

The prophet Isaiah, Amos' successor, developed the theme,
as did Jeremiah after him:

> Thus said the Lord, the King of Israel,
> Their Redeemer, the Lord of Hosts:
> I am the first and I am the last,
> And there is no god but Me.
> Who like Me can announce,
> Can foretell it—and match Me thereby?
> Even as I told the future to an ancient people,
> So let him foretell coming events to them.
> > Isa. 44:6–7

> O Lord, there is none like You!
> You are great and Your name is great in power.
> Who would not revere You, O King of the nations?
> For that is Your due,
> Since among all the wise of the nations
> And among all their royalty
> There is none like You.
> > Jer. 10:6–7

This was indeed a totally new conception of God. It should
come as no great surprise that it was not the most popular

idea of its time. It was not appreciated by the more powerful nations surrounding Israel. It is remarkable that this idea of One Universal God not only survived through the centuries, but that today it has become accepted by almost all people and all nations, at least as the ideal.

All nations are subject to and judged by the same moral law. One nation cannot claim to have done no wrong if, for example, it has ever murdered innocent people. If, under the moral law of the One Universal God, it is considered wrong to take innocent life, then any and all nations which so act are guilty and subject to judgment and punishment by other nations. If, under the moral law of the One Universal God, it is considered wrong to take the territory of one's neighbor, or to deny another group its freedom, then a nation which tries to do this is morally wrong and subject to the judgment and punishment of the rest of the nations that have submitted to that international code. It was precisely on this theory that the Allies tried (and convicted) the leaders of a defeated Nazi Germany after World War II. The Nuremberg Trials were based on this old prophetic idea.

Here are three of the principles of the Nuremberg Trials:

1. Any person who commits an act which constitutes a crime under international law is responsible and liable to punishment.
2. The fact that a person who committed an act which constitutes a crime under international law while acting as Head of State or as a responsible government official does not relieve him/her from responsibility under international law.
3. The fact that a person acted pursuant to orders of his/her government or a superior does not relieve him/her from responsibility under international law, provided a moral choice was in fact possible.

The prophets went even further. They believed that God would even use other nations to punish Israel for violations of international moral conduct. Can you imagine how shocking such ideas must have been for the people of Israel to whom the prophets addressed their words?

But whose law was to become the international standard? Whose god was to become supreme? The god of the Babylonians? The god of the Egyptians? The god and the law of the Assyrians? Naturally, the prophets believed that it was to be *their* God and *their* God's law that would eventually triumph and be recognized by the peoples of the world. It did not occur to the prophets that the other nations might not accept the claim of the law of the God of Israel, but they were not so foolish as to believe that what they dreamed of and yearned for would occur easily or even in their lifetimes. Therefore, they spoke also of preserving the independence of the nation of Israel. A nation's existence, its right to protect itself from conquest, must be maintained until the great time of messianic peace. And therein lies the difficulty, the conflict between nationalism (my nation first) and internationalism (world cooperation).

The prophets opposed militarism as a false pride and a denial of trust in God, but they certainly did not want to see the nation of Israel disappear or be absorbed into another society's culture. How to resist, in order to preserve their identity, was a difficult matter. The prophets believed that military resistance to the more powerful nations that surrounded Israel was futile. Hosea believed that the people would be saved by God's compassion rather than by the bow, the sword, and battle (Hos. 1:7). Isaiah warned King Ahaz against any entangling alliances with foreign powers (Isa. 7). The prophets' advice ran against the grain of the people's will and behavior at that time.

In simple terms, the people of Israel were not pacifists, rejecting violence under all circumstances—and they practiced war. However, as no other people of their day, they struggled intensely with the ethical questions of war: What kind of a war was right, what kind was not? Who should go to war and who could remain home and avoid serving in the military? What was proper conduct for soldiers? What was humane and what was the army not allowed to do to its enemies because it was wrong? History does not show that any other nation of the ancient world dealt with the problem of war with as much sensitivity as the ancient people of Israel.

In the biblical period, 250 years before the prophets, war was accepted as a correct instrument of foreign policy. Israel had its own manual of war. It is found in the twentieth chapter of Deuteronomy. It is a fascinating document. As you read it, notice the following:

> a. the categories of those who are excused from the army and the reasons why.
> b. what must be done to an enemy's city before beginning a siege or an attack against it.
> c. rules for taking booty.
> d. the use of the *cherem;* the total destruction of all living things in a besieged community.
> e. the rules governing the destruction of trees.
> f. the appointment of a military chaplain.
> g. the rules that govern war with cities "that lie very far from you" (nations outside the boundaries of Canaan) and those governing "war with cities which the Lord your God is giving you as a heritage" (the inhabitants of Canaan).
> h. the rules governing the taking of a female captive. See chap. 21:10–14.

Two kinds of military conduct are described in Deuteronomy. Later the rabbis, who refined and interpreted the biblical material, outlined two different kinds of warfare: the necessary war, called in Hebrew, *Milchemet Mitzvah,* and the optional war, called *Milchemet Reshut.* The Bible tells us that the Israelites were instructed to destroy utterly the

heathen nations of Canaan whom they encountered and
fought against as they sought to conquer and settle the land
"lest they mislead you into doing all the abhorrent things
that they have done for their gods and you stand guilty
before the Lord your God" (Deut. 20:18). In other words,
these groups were to be totally wiped out so that their pagan
ideas and their idolatry could not infect and corrupt the
people of Israel. This total destruction is known in Hebrew
as exercising the *cherem,* the ban. From the viewpoint of
our day, it seems like a cruel and barbaric way to conduct
war, for not only are the male soldiers killed, but also
women, children, cattle—indeed all living things in the
community. One cannot read these verses without thinking
of the atomic destruction of Nagasaki and Hiroshima, which
ended World War II, or of the saturation bombing of the
German city of Dresden during the war.

One can explain and understand the use of the cherem
without trying to justify it. The nations of Canaan, and those
others to be totally destroyed by the Israelites, were known
in Hebrew literature as *Amalek* – the name of the tribe that
engaged in an unprovoked attack on the rear of the Israelite
camp as it travelled through the desert out of Egypt (see
Exod. 17:8–16 and Deut. 25:17–19). These nations were those
against whom a necessary war could be waged on two
grounds: in self-defense, or if the enemy nation was judged
to be totally evil. That raises some interesting questions. Can
we call Hitler and Nazi Germany Amalek? What about the
Arabs? Would the modern State of Israel be justified in waging an atomic war against the Arab nations that surround
her and threaten her life?

The great philosopher, Martin Buber, once wrote: "I
have never been able to believe that this is a message of
God. . . . Nothing can make me believe in a God who
punishes Saul because he has not murdered his enemy."
(Autobiographical fragments translated by Maurice Friedman in *The Philosophy of Martin Buber,* The Open Court
Publishing Company, 1965.)

The rabbis were troubled by the harshness of the cherem exercised in a Milchemet Mitzvah, and they sought to soften its usage. Noting the instruction in Deut. 20:10–11, where the leader is ordered first to "offer ... terms of peace" to the besieged community, the rabbis declared that peace is to be offered even to the archenemies of Israel on condition that they accept the "seven commandments enjoined upon the descendants of Noah." These laws were (1) not to worship idols; (2) not to blaspheme the name of God; (3) to establish courts of justice; (4) not to kill; (5) not to commit adultery; (6) not to rob; and (7) not to eat flesh cut from a living animal.

The idea of a Milchemet Reshut, or optional war, came from the biblical description of the way war was to be conducted against the nations "very far from you," outside the land of Canaan. Such a war, the rabbis said, was one waged to extend the borders of Israel or to enhance the greatness of the ruling monarch. A decision to engage in an optional war could not be made by the king alone. It had to be approved by the Sanhedrin, the collective leadership of the people. The idea in this instance was that there was less excuse for an optional war, and that the thinking of the elders would limit occasions for that war. Under the United States Constitution, even a war of self-defense first has to be authorized by the Congress. One of the major objections raised by peace groups to America's engaging in the Vietnam War was that it was never authorized by Congress and, therefore, it was as illegal as it was immoral. Investigate the history of our nation's intervention in Vietnam, and determine whether you think that war was a Milchemet Mitzvah or a Milchemet Reshut.

While the biblical lawmakers, and later the rabbis, all agreed that a war was obligatory when the people were attacked in their own land by an outside force, they were not so unified in their attitude toward what today is called a "preemptive war"—that is, one that is initiated to *prevent* attack. The famous Six Day War, launched against Egypt and Syria by Israel in 1967, was that kind of war. Egypt had moved 100,000 soldiers and hundreds of tanks to the Sinai border, and Israel was convinced that an attack was about to occur, and that she might be overrun. So Israel initiated the war. It proved to be a decisive and smashing victory.

As a result of that daring initiative, much land that had been lost to the Arabs in 1948 was recaptured by Israel, as was the eastern section of the old city of Jerusalem. The city fell once again into Jewish hands and was unified.

Was the Six Day War a Milchemet Mitzvah or a Milchemet Reshut? Modern rabbinical authorities still debate the point. Most Jews, however, would agree that it was an obligatory war. What do you think?

Can a Jew be a conscientious objector? Can a Jew be a pacifist?

The answer to these questions is yes.

There are and there have always been Jewish pacifists, people who deeply believe that war can never be morally or ethically justified. There is even a small organization in America called the Jewish Peace Fellowship, created by Jewish pacifists. They believe it is better to be killed than to kill, that war is always a sin against God's unity and against the divine nature of all people, that nonviolent resistance is morally preferable to organized murder. It is doubtful that a modern nation could survive with such a faith, but pacifists believe that they have a right to say no to the state when it seeks their participation in war. They believe that Judaism and Jewish history justify their position.

The great hero of Jewish pacifism was Jochanan ben Zakkai. He was a rabbi who lived in the first century of the Common Era. He was convinced that Jewish resistance to Rome was futile. He begged the Roman Emperor Vespasian, who at that time was directing the assault on Jerusalem, to let him found a school outside of Jerusalem for the study of Torah, and to establish a *bet din* (court of justice). The emperor granted his request, and ben Zakkai's school became the leading academy of the Jewish world. It also saved Judaism after the bulk of the Jewish community was destroyed by the Roman military. The teachers of Torah, the scholars trained there, became the seed bed from which Judaism again sprouted. The Jewish people survived, not by force of arms, but through the study and observance of the Torah, and by devoted commitment to their historic faith. It is another powerful example of the truth of the words of the prophet Zechariah:

> Not by might, nor by power,
> but by My spirit, said the Lord of Hosts.
>
> Zech. 4.6

Jewish pacifists point to the biblical tradition to strengthen their position. They also point out the obvious truth that wars do not solve international problems. They only create new and bigger ones in their wake. War breeds war, and each succeeding war is more destructive than the one before. War is an evil which runs counter to the will of God, since it is destructive of life and society. The right of a person to be a pacifist has been recognized by most societies through the granting of conscientious objector status to those who in conscience cannot participate.

In Israel, every able-bodied man and woman (except women excused on religious grounds) must serve in the military. Do you think the government of Israel should exempt those who, in conscience or because they are disheartened, ask not to serve?

The United States government allows for conscientious objection. Originally, the law exempted persons from military service who, by reason of religious training and belief, conscientiously opposed participating in war *in any form.* The law defined "religious training and belief" as a person's belief in the Supreme Being, involving duties superior to those arising from any human relation. However, a recent constitutional amendment allows exemption from military service for those who hold profound moral convictions against war. Belief in a Supreme Being is no longer the only basis on which one can claim conscientious objector status. Thus a nonreligious person can also be a pacifist.

Although the issue of selective conscientious objection (refusal to fight in a particular war) was never dealt with specifically in Jewish sources, the spirit of our tradition supports such a category. The Bible exempts those who are "afraid and disheartened" out of concern for the harmful influence they might have on other soldiers.

> The officials shall go on addressing the troops and say, "Is there anyone afraid and disheartened? Let him go back to his home, lest the courage of his comrades flag like his."
>
> Deut. 20:8

The Mishnah comments on this verse:

> Rabbi Akiba says: "Fearful and fainthearted" ["Afraid and disheartened"] is to be understood literally—he cannot endure the armies joined in battle or bear to see a drawn sword. Rabbi Jose the Galilean says: "Fearful and fainthearted" alludes to one who is afraid because of the transgressions he had committed.
>
> Sotah 44a

The Gemara, in turn, expands on the Mishnah:

> Our rabbis taught: If he heard the sound of trumpets and was terrorstricken, or beheld the brandishing of swords and the urine discharged itself upon his knees, he returns home.
>
> Sotah 44b

It appears that the rabbis were concerned about not forcing military service on those who, by virtue of character or disposition, were unfit to serve.

There are rabbinic sources that instruct people to allow themselves to be killed, rather than follow orders to commit murder. Also, the Mishnah reminds us that to kill one person is like destroying the entire world. Jewish justification for selective conscientious objection seems quite strong.

LIMITS OF WAR

Over and above the question of an individual's right not to fight is the question of moral limits on waging a war. The conduct of war was as important to the ancient Israelites as was the decision over whether or not to engage in a war, or who was expected to fight. Here, as in all other war-peace issues, the overarching concerns had to do with how to cause the least rather than the greatest amount of suffering. Even in those days of primitive weapons and limited capacity to kill, people knew that "war is hell" and that fighting brutalized those who engaged in it.

After the Six Day War, an Israeli soldier wrote a moving account of how the soldiers with whom he served were influenced by this ancient prohibition:*

> In my company, we had a religious C.O. from Kibbutz *Tirat Zvi*. On the first day, after we'd gone through Jenin, we moved on to the objective and found all the Jordanians had gone. We dug ourselves in there because there were reports that they might mount a mortar barrage, and we stayed there until later that night. Then we went down into the village. While we were up there the administrative personnel had gone into the village. When we got to the base, we found the storekeepers and the cooks—all that lot —absolutely rolling in things that they'd looted from the village. Wrapped up in carpets, women's jewelry—it was a horrible scene. At that moment, everybody thought: for God's sake, what do they need all that stuff for? Then, I remember, the C.O. got the whole company together,

*Henry Near, ed., *The Seventh Day: Soldiers Talk about the Six Day War* (New York: Charles Scribner's Sons, 1970), pp. 126–127.

formed them all up in a semicircle and stuck all the store-keepers and cooks in the middle along with their loot. Then he started quoting them chapter and verse of the Bible: "Thou shalt not plunder. Thou shalt not . . . Thou shalt not. . . ." It was really impressive. After he'd finished, one of the storekeepers got up and asked him, "What about that bit in the Bible 'And when Jehosaphat and his men came to take away the spoil,' what do you make of that, then?" So the C.O. began to explain that Rashi, comment-ing on the verse, says that it should be taken to mean that a conquering army takes only what it really needs during the fighting. That's to say, if they have no food, and since they have to live somehow, then they take what they need, but nothing more than that—no property. I stood in a cor-ner and I thought to myself, "What a peculiar army this is, standing there and listening to all this stuff." But there was something to it.

It would be wrong to pretend that Israel always lives up to the prophetic standard of shalom. In its occupation of Arab lands, its furious reprisals against terrorism, its treatment of Israeli Arabs, its attitude toward Palestinian aspirations, its reluctance to take additional risks for peace—Israel func-tions like most nation-states. Should Israel be held to a higher standard? The standard of God's Chosen People?

Nuclear Super Powers

Since both the United States and the Soviet Union have developed nuclear arsenals that can incinerate the world in the twinkling of an eye, into what category would a nuclear war be placed? "Does the right to self-defense include the right to destroy with the push of a button millions and per-haps billions of persons both in the land of the enemy and in one's own land?" (Richard G. Hirsch, *Thy Most Precious Gift*, UAHC, page 50.)

Isn't nuclear war, by its very nature, immoral? But if it

is immoral, is not the failure to defend against it equally immoral?

This tragic impasse may yet drive humanity to suicide and, if not that, to such economic impoverishment, that nations will have too few resources left for needed life support, life-giving policies and programs. It is the kind of end-of-days nightmare that the prophet Jeremiah foresaw when he lamented:

> Oh, my suffering, my suffering!
> How I writhe!
> Oh, the walls of my heart!
> My heart moans within me,
> I cannot be silent;
> For I hear the blare of horns,
> Alarms of war.
> Disaster overtakes disaster,
> For all the land has been ravaged,
> Suddenly my tents have been ravaged,
> In a moment, my tent cloths.
>
> Jer. 4:19–20

> My people are stupid,
> They give Me no heed;
> They are foolish children,
> They are not intelligent.
> They are clever at doing wrong,
> But unable to do right.
>
> Jer. 4:22

Each year the United States spends over one hundred billion dollars, or 25 percent of its national budget for defense, including nuclear weapons. Is it money well spent, or should we considerably reduce the expenditure? This question is always hotly debated by the American people. Some argue that so long as the Soviet Union continues to seek nuclear superiority over us, we have no choice. If we fall behind, they will dominate us. Others say that talk about military superiority is a false issue. The former secretary of state,

Henry Kissinger, once said: "What in God's name do you do with military superiority?" As one historian has observed:

> The period of American monopoly of the bomb was the period of greatest Soviet pushfulness in foreign policy, of the rapid satellitization of Eastern Europe and of the Communist conquest of China. "Nuclear superiority" of the United States did not deter the Korean War or the Berlin blockade. In short, "nuclear superiority" was irrelevant to the political and military struggles of the immediate postwar world. Its primary effect was to spur the Soviets to catch up.
>
> Richard Barnet, "Promise of Disarmament,"
> *New York Times Magazine,* February 27, 1977

Those who oppose the continued rise in military spending point out that both superpowers already possess enough nuclear armament to wipe each other out immediately and that "inflicting 40 million casualties on an enemy and suffering 20 million yourself is not a political definition of 'winning.'" Superiority is not only meaningless, it is unattainable. What we ought to be doing is building our true strength. "A United States dedicated to strengthening its economy, extending its democracy and facing its real security problems—world starvation, nuclear proliferation, exhaustion of energy resources and the contamination of basic life support systems—has no reason to fear the Soviet stockpile, even if it were as large as our own" (Barnet, p. 55).

The same thought was expressed by the rabbis centuries ago when they observed that the Hebrew word for war, *milchamah,* is related to the word for bread, *lechem.* Bread, or lack of it, is literally at the root of war. As often as not, the seeds of war are to be found in the inability of a nation to sustain its people with adequate food and shelter. Persistent world poverty may well lead the world to another and perhaps totally destructive war. Two-thirds of the people of the world are poor and hungry. It is impossible to maintain a stable world with that kind of imbalance.

The attitude is reflected in the difference between peace and the Hebrew word used for peace, shalom.

Peace, according to the dictionary, is "the absence of a state of war." Shalom, on the other hand, is translated as the presence of something positive; it can be translated as completeness, wholeness, perfection, welfare, security, salvation, or rest. Shalom is not a negative term, not an absence, but a positive presence. Shalom requires more than a balance of power or terror, more than a state of disarmament. Shalom is a condition of human harmony on an international level founded on the well-being of nations and the personal well-being of individuals.

In *Pirkei Avot,* a rabbinic work, we learn:

> The sword comes into the world because of justice being delayed, because of justice being perverted, and because of those who teach the law not according to halachah.
>
> Avot 5:12

Let us hope that this lesson will help us in our own lives to speed the cause of justice and peace—shalom.

XI

Individual Responsibility

"GREASERS, damn them anyway! Wops and niggers! They all stink!" Frank muttered as he slid into his chair beside his buddy, Nat, in English class. Frank was mad, steaming mad. But it wasn't until after class that Nat found out what had happened to cause Frank to explode in such a terrible rage.

Nat liked Frank a lot. Frank had what Nat's dad always called *sechel,* common sense. He was a leader, not a follower. He was independent, thought clearly, and, most of all, he didn't usually fly off the handle. This kind of outburst from Frank was so unusual that it left Nat stunned. Besides, both the boys had lots of non-Jewish friends in school including, among others, blacks, Puerto Ricans, Italians, and Poles.

The trouble had erupted on the stairs between the second and third floors. Frank was in a hurry and he didn't see the others at first. But they were there, blocking him as he tried to step past. One was a black, an upper classman whom Frank didn't know. The other seemed to be one of those boys who act tough and who come from that part of the community which has a heavy Italian and Slovak population. Frank didn't recognize him either. He suspected he didn't even go to the school.

"That'll be four bits, buster, if you want to leave these stairs in one piece."

It happened every day in the school; younger and smaller students were being shaken down by older and tougher ones. Everyone in the school—students and teachers—knew it was going on, but seemed afraid to do anything about it. The students either paid up and shut up or tried to avoid being where the others were. It was one of those situations where all seemed to look the other way. Those who were involved did not even tell their parents about it. It was another one of life's little irritants that the majority learned to tolerate. Some of the young people even brought an extra quarter or two with them to school, just in case. One Jewish girl jokingly referred to the collection as Keren Ami.

Until that day, Frank had been lucky. He hadn't been bothered. But that day his luck ran out and he hadn't liked it. It was his last half-dollar, and he just didn't like being ripped off. He said so in no uncertain terms, to the two hoods who stopped him. The two-against-one fight that followed would have certainly ended with Frank on the floor nursing a couple of painful bruises, at least, or maybe something worse, had it not been for the sudden appearance of Mrs. Pederson, the art teacher. The toughs went quickly through a door at the top of the stairs and disappeared down the corridor.

Frank brushed off Mrs. Pederson's questions and headed for his class. It was just another incident. But then Frank boiled over in justifiable fury.

A couple of things troubled Nat. First, there was the unveiled bigotry of his friend's outburst. But second, and even more disturbing, the thought grew inside Nat that the hateful things which Frank had spat out in anger were words he had also said to himself. Not only had he been hit a couple of times in a similar way, but he also remembered the times when friends of his had their bikes or sleds "liberated" in the park by a small gang and, in each instance, the kids involved were either black or of the "greaser" variety. Moreover, he had heard his parents talking about how "they" had made the city unsafe at night, about how "they" constituted over 80 percent of the prison population, about how "they" dominated the drug and prostitution business.

He saw himself falling into a trap, the trap of *stereotyping*, condemning all members of a group, race, or class because of the actions of a few. He didn't like what he was thinking. He didn't like what he saw himself becoming. Was he himself a bigot? Was his friend Frank a bigot?

Besides, he asked himself, is it right to blame an entire race or group because of the rotten behavior of a few? Isn't that what anti-Semites do to Jews? It seems never to work in reverse. We don't praise an entire group when one of their members does something outstanding. No one says that all Americans are brilliant scientists and writers because five Americans won Nobel prizes in science and literature in 1976.

Why should all people of a specific group be condemned or made to suffer because of the evils that some in that group may do? Doesn't the individual count for something?

GRANDPA AND THE GERMANS

Nat remembered a conversation he once had with his grandfather. It wasn't exactly a conversation, since his grandfather had gotten so emotional during the discussion that Nat decided it was better to try to keep quiet. But, of course, he didn't succeed.

It began when Nat first asked about the number he saw tattooed on his grandfather's arm. It was then that he learned that Grandpa had been in a Nazi concentration camp during World War II. His grandfather told him how the Germans had tattooed that number onto his arm before loading him, his wife, and family into a box car, and shipping them to a camp deep inside Poland. His grandfather, Nat learned, was the only one in the entire family to survive. The rest were killed by the Nazis. It was a horrible story and, even though more than 35 years had passed, tears had come to his grandfather's eyes as he told his grandson a little of what had happened. It was the first time Nat had ever seen an adult cry uncontrollably, and he never forgot that moment. He also remembered that his grandfather said he would never stop hating the German people.

As Nat grew older, he began to argue with his grandfather about his hatred of Germans. One argument went like this:

"But, Grandpa," he had said, *"all* Germans couldn't be bad. Besides, that was a long time ago. There are thousands of Germans living in Germany today who weren't even born during the time of Hitler. They don't hate Jews. We have a girl in our class who just came from Germany and she told me that after the war the German government gave Israel millions of dollars to help Israel get started, and that even today Jewish survivors of the Nazis receive money from the German government. If that's so, they can't all be bad. She told us a lot about how many young Germans today help Israel, how many of them visit Israel, and how well Jews live who are still in Germany. As a matter of fact, Grandpa, I'd like to go to Germany when I grow up just to see it. I don't hate the Germans. You can't blame them for what their parents and grandparents did."

It was at that point that his grandfather blew up.

"How can you say that, knowing all they did to me and to your family? They murdered six million Jews, wiped out the Jewish population of Germany for no reason other than the fact that they were Jews. And you try to tell me they're not all *bad?* Do you know what it takes to kill six million people? Even if the entire population of Germany didn't participate, surely they must have known what was going on. And imagine how many "good" Germans must have been a part of that! You speak of individuals, Nat. Where were the individuals who could have stood up and protested? Where were the church leaders, the intellectuals from the universities, the labor leaders, the writers, the social thinkers? I'll tell you where they were: they were silent and afraid. Maybe some of them were bothered by what they saw happening, but they didn't have the courage to protest. Can you imagine that happening in this country?"

"No, I can't," Nat replied.

"Why didn't the Germans rise up in revolt? Germans, ah, they're no good. They never were. And let me tell you something, my boy, they never will be."

Nat felt trapped. His grandfather's strong feeling was driving him into a corner. Besides, somehow the argument had gotten twisted around. Nat hadn't intended to defend Hitler or to apologize for the Germans who did wrong. He had also read about the American atomic bombing of the Japanese cities of Hiroshima and Nagasaki in World War II and had wondered to himself about the killing of hundreds of thousands of innocent Japanese civilians. Was that wrong, too? Did that make all Americans murderers? Are we barbaric, too? He tried to raise a different, though related, question. *Should an entire people be condemned for the misdeeds of some?*

Two separate but related problems were now tangled in Nat's head as he walked home:

a. the stereotyping of a race or group because of the actions of some members of that group; and

b.the condemnation of an entire people because of the sins of those who lived before them.

Questions whirled in Nat's head:

Where does the individual fit into all this? Is Frank right? I know I can trust Tom, my black friend, but how far can I trust his black friends whom I don't know? And what about Ilse? Do I turn away from her because some of her relatives 35 years ago may have been Nazis who either killed, or permitted the destruction of, members of my family? How should I feel about Germans today? Should they be made to feel guilty for events that occurred in their country before most of them were even born? Should Jews visit Germany or buy German-made products? He smiled as he

thought about this last question, knowing how many of his
Jewish friends' parents owned Mercedes Benzes and Volks-
wagens.

Without knowing it, Nat had involved himself in one of
humanity's, and Judaism's, most difficult problems. It was as
old as Abraham, and it has snarled the individual's relations
to others—and to God—from the beginning to the present.

ABRAHAM AND GOD

Do you know the story of Abraham's bargaining with God?
The story is found in Genesis, chapter 18. As the Bible describes it, God decided to destroy the two cities of Sodom
and Gomorrah because of their sinfulness. He notified
Abraham of the plan. Abraham came to the defense of the
two communities and their inhabitants. "Will you sweep
away the innocent along with the guilty?" he demanded of
God. "What if there should be 50 innocent within the city;
will You then wipe out the place and not forgive it for the
sake of the innocent 50 who are in it?" God answered that
the cities would not be destroyed if 50 innocent persons
could be found. And if there are 45? Yes, God responded, I
will save the communities if there are 45 decent people to
be found. And so the bargaining continued until Abraham
wrung from God a promise not to destroy Sodom and
Gomorrah if even ten innocent persons were found. As it
turned out, not even ten such persons could be found in the
two cities and God did indeed cause both of the cities to be
burned to the ground. But that is not the point.

The point is that for the first time the biblical writers
dealt with the problem of whether the innocent should be
punished with the guilty. God is portrayed as a merciful
judge who would spare the guilty for the sake of the innocent, or, to put the matter more positively, the entire group
would not be condemned because of some evil persons in
their midst. This was the principle of *individual responsi-*

bility, which the prophets of Israel were later to develop.

There is no denying the fact that a society does bear the responsibility for and frequently suffers from the misdeeds of individuals in its midst. It may not be right, but it is a fact of our lives. The insurance rates for automobile drivers younger than twenty-five are much higher than the rates for those over twenty-five, because it is a statistical fact that more drivers under twenty-five are involved in accidents than those over that age. Auto insurance on males under twenty-five is higher than the same kind of insurance for females, again because the statistics show that more males are involved in accidents than females in that age group. Poor, black, and Puerto Rican young males are viewed with suspicion in some large cities because it is a fact that more youthful criminals in large cities are black or Puerto Rican. Poverty, discrimination, bad education, and lack of jobs lead many to hopelessness and crime. This, however, does not and should not lead to the conclusion that all or even most black or Puerto Rican young males are criminals. Recently in Crown Heights, a section of New York City, a group of Chasidic Jews beat up a couple of black young people. Does this make all Chasidim thugs? Are all white young males bums because six whites with baseball bats beat a group of joggers in Central Park?

Frank's anger clouded his thinking to such a degree that he made a false conclusion about *all* blacks or Italians from the particular experience he had with two. And Frank had made it worse by uttering racial slurs, which is no different from branding Jews "kikes" and "yids."

JOSHUA AND ACHAN

The Bible has an interesting account of how an entire society was held responsible for the misdeed of one member of that society. According to the Book of Joshua, after Moses died and Joshua became the leader of the people, he led them across the Jordan and began to conquer the cities and towns on the east bank of the Jordan. One of those cities was Ai. Joshua sent spies ahead to see how well fortified Ai was and how many warriors would be needed to capture it. The spies returned with a report that only a small force would be necessary to conquer it. Joshua followed the recommendation and, much to his surprise, the Hebrews were thoroughly beaten by the inhabitants.

Joshua then complained to the Lord: "Ah, Lord God!" cried Joshua. "Why did you lead this people across the Jordan only to deliver us into the hands of the Amorites, to be destroyed by them?" God told Joshua that his attack force was routed because the people of Israel had sinned. "They have taken of the proscribed and put it in their vessels; they have stolen; they have broken faith." Joshua was shocked. He had no idea that this had happened. By a process of investigation outlined to him by God, he discovered the culprit. Achan, son of Carmi, had stolen "a fine Shinar mantle, two hundred shekels of silver, and a wedge of gold weighing fifty shekels," and he had buried the loot in the floor of his tent. Punishment followed quickly. It was as severe as it was swift. Achan was first stoned to death by the community; then the gold and silverware were burned, together with his corpse, his sons, daughters, oxen, asses, sheep, tent, and all he had. Not only did the larger community suffer from Achan's crime in that they lost a battle and 36 of their warriors were killed, but Achan's immediate family paid for his crime with their lives (Josh., Chapter 7).

These notions of guilt by association and collective responsibility, where the entire community is held responsible for the misdeeds of one or a few of its members, are found frequently in the biblical literature. Was God cruel? How could a merciful God do such a horrible thing?

King David complained bitterly about such punishment. In a story found in 2 Sam. 24:17, David acknowledged his own guilt in a situation, but protested against the Lord's also destroying innocent people with a plague. Such punishment must have been the common practice of the period—so common, in fact, that the so-called Deuteronomic Code makes it illegal to punish children for the sins of their parents:

> Parents shall not be put to death for children, nor children be put to death for parents: a person shall be put to death only for his own crime.
>
> Deut. 24:16

JEREMIAH AND INDIVIDUAL RESPONSIBILITY

The prophet Jeremiah also dealt with this problem. Remember, Jeremiah lived during that terrible period immediately before, during, and after the captivity of the Jewish people by Babylon and their exile to that country. Many of those taken into exile considered themselves innocent of any wrongdoing, victims of a situation which they didn't create. What had they done to deserve being uprooted from their homes and their land, forced into exile in a new and strange country? The people felt that they were innocent victims of a situation inherited from their parents. They were not to blame. However, Jeremiah did not accept their effort to shift the blame to earlier generations. Much of his prophetic life had been given over to warning the people of the impending disaster precisely because *they* had failed to fulfill the demands of ethical relationships. But Jeremiah was not the "I told you so" type. To him, God's purpose was not to overthrow or to destroy the people. According to Jeremiah, God wanted the restoration of the people as much as they wanted it for themselves. He dreamed of a time when God would make a new covenant with the people of Israel, not like the old one but one which would be written upon their hearts. That was his way of saying that he longed for the time when people would no longer have to be taught good behavior—they would be born with a knowledge of it and would act accordingly:

> In those days, they shall no longer say, "Fathers have eaten sour grapes and children's teeth are blunted." But everyone shall die for his own sins: whosoever eats sour grapes, his teeth shall be blunted.
>
> (Jer. 31:29–30)

Jeremiah has often been called the prophet of individual religion. That does not mean that Jeremiah glorified the image of the rugged individualist who lived by a private religious faith, credo, and set of rules, unmindful of the rest of society. To the contrary, Jeremiah knew the value of society. He knew that people had to live in community and that, especially in times of tragedy or social upheaval, people needed one another. The new covenant, of which he spoke, was intended for the community—the house of Israel and the house of Judah—but he also knew that a community was shaped by what its individuals did or did not do. A community was no better than the values of its members. He prayed with all his heart for a community of people, each one of whom would be fashioned with a new heart, and would see what was demanded and do it, so that the whole house of Israel might live. He wanted to put an end once and for all to the injustice of having the many suffer for the sins of a few, and to the equally unfair situation in which individuals were forced to pay the price for the misdeeds of those who came before them.

EZEKIEL AND GOD'S JUSTICE

Ezekiel was forced to deal with the problem of individual responsibility from a different angle. He lived and prophesied only in Babylonia, a community already in exile. Naturally, the Jews in Babylonia were quite bitter about

what had happened to them. Many had grown cynical about
God, religion, the future. One can almost hear them saying:
God is not fair, punishing us with this exile for sins our
parents committed. What's the use? God is either powerless
or cruel. Why believe in God? Why believe in anything?
Why be good? Ezekiel challenged those who thought that
way. We have a record of that confrontation in Ezekiel,
chapter 18:

> The word of the Lord came to me: What do you mean by
> quoting this proverb upon the soil of Israel, "Fathers eat
> sour grapes and their children's teeth are blunted"? As I
> live—declares the Lord God—this proverb shall no longer
> be current among you in Israel. Consider, all lives are
> Mine; the life of the father and the life of the son are both
> Mine. The person who sins, only he shall die.
>
> Ezek. 18:1-4

His words cut through the cynicism like a knife through soft
butter. The acts of past generations neither determine the
response of the present generation nor shape their future.
Each individual person is to be judged on the basis of what
he or she does. All individuals are responsible for their own
destinies. People are neither the victims nor the captives of
what those who came before them did. They must answer
for themselves, to God and others, and for no one else. No
longer could they shift the blame to others or to earlier
generations.

Ezekiel made his point even more dramatically in the
rest of that famous chapter. Good parents do not necessarily
produce good children. The parent shall not be blamed or
suffer for the sins of the child. The child shall suffer for his
or her own mistakes. Conversely, a wicked parent may produce a righteous child. That child shall not be asked to answer for the parent. Only "the person who sins . . . shall die."
Ezekiel goes further: Why would God want it otherwise?
Does God take some delight in the death of even a wicked

person? Do you think God is that cruel, that vengeful? If that were God's nature, God would not be God. No! God takes no pleasure in the death of any person, especially not an evil one. That may be a human characteristic: it is not one of God's.

> Is it my desire that a wicked man shall die?—says the Lord God. It is rather that he shall turn back from his ways and live.
>
> Ezek. 18:23

> Cast away all the transgressions by which you have offended, and get yourselves a new heart and a new spirit, that you may not die, O House of Israel. For it is not My desire that anyone shall die—declares the Lord God. Repent, therefore, and live!
>
> Ezek. 18:31–32

With this, Ezekiel introduced the idea of repentance, *te-shuvah*. The word in Hebrew comes from the root *shuv*, meaning "to return." It is one of Judaism's most important concepts. Stated simply, it suggests that no person is condemned by the past, nor should be judged by it. Moreover, even if a person has done wrong, one is not forever condemned by it. People can and do change. They can choose to be different. In other words, people have free will. The whole idea of teshuvah in Judaism is based on the idea that people have the capacity to choose freely to change the direction of their lives. They are not destined, either by forces outside themselves or by their own natures, to a particular course of action or life-style. And how is the change affected? By a decision, by an act of the mind and will. The prophet Hosea put it this way:

> Return, O Israel, to the Lord your God,
> For you have fallen because of your sin.
> Take words with you
> And return to the Lord.
>
> Hos. 14:2–3

When the prophet used the phrase "take words with you" what he meant was "say to yourselves" that you will try to do and be better.

Did you ever realize that this idea is the essence of our two most important holy days, Rosh Hashanah and Yom Kippur? Certainly you must have asked yourself: Why do Jews spend a whole day in the synagogue, reciting prayers? What is the *purpose* of these two days? It should be to help us think seriously about what we have done (and not done) during the past year, and to resolve to do things differently and better during the year to come. On Yom Kippur, the Torah portion that is read in Reform synagogues is taken from Deuteronomy and ends with the command to the people:

> Choose life—if you and your offspring would live.
>
> Deut. 30:19

Take a minute to read all of Deuteronomy, chapter 30. You will see clearly how the people who wrote the Bible believed that individuals had the capacity to direct the course of their own lives. It's a wonderful and challenging vision of the nature of people.

But—we know that, unfortunately, life is not always like that. After all, people *do* suffer for the mistakes and wrong choices of those who lived before them. In this sense, the children's teeth *are* blunted because of the sour grapes their parents ate. If we can't swim in a lake or use a beach today that 50 years ago was free of pollution; if we can't fish in a stream that 25 years ago was teeming with trout; if the air of our cities is so filled with fumes and chemicals that our eyes water, or we have trouble breathing on certain days— it isn't *our* fault, is it? "They" did it to us years ago. The problems our generation has with the environment are the result of the "sour grapes" our ancestors "ate" before we were even born. That is all quite true. But what is equally true is that we have the freedom and the capacity to reverse that process—if we want to, if we care enough, if we have the will. And the truth is that, even today, knowing all we do about how one generation affects the lives of unborn generations, too many of us still don't care, still say "Oh, what's the use?" We shirk our responsibilities, turn our backs, hide from the problems, surrender our individual responsibility.

Here is a stark example of where that leads:

Some years ago, in Kew Gardens, New York, a young woman named Kitty Genovese, coming home at 3:00 A.M. from work as a waitress, was stalked by a murderer who stabbed her in three separate attacks over a period of *30 minutes.* During that harrowing period, the young victim screamed desperately for help. Thirty-eight persons heard the screams; a few actually looked out their windows and watched the bloody scene unfold on the streets. *Not one of them did anything. Nobody went to her aid. Nobody called the police.* Kitty Genovese was killed by a crazed man, but also by ordinary citizens who became silent accomplices to the foul deed.

How could people behave like that? What possible reasons could there be? Newspaper reporters interviewed the people to find out. Most of them said, they didn't want to get involved. It would have been dangerous to go down to the street and confront a murderer, but why didn't they merely call the police? They didn't want to get involved. The police would have come around to bother them; maybe they would have had to be witnesses at a trial. Why be a good Samaritan? The girl wasn't related to them; they didn't know her. What was she doing out at such an ungodly hour anyway? Besides, it was the middle of the night; they were entitled to their sleep, were they not? So they behaved as if they were watching a violent television show, after which they could turn off the dial and go to sleep. But it wasn't a television fantasy: a fellow human being was dying—and they couldn't get involved.

Was the Kitty Genovese case a special situation? In that

same year, in Albany, New York, a mentally ill youth climbed on a ledge of the roof of a hotel, and threatened to leap to his death. A large crowd gathered beneath the hotel, and they urged him to jump. "Chicken!" and "Yellow!" they bellowed at him.

Commenting on the Albany incident, an editorial in *The New York Times* asked: "Are they any different from the wild-eyed Romans watching and cheering as men and beasts tore each other apart in the Colosseum [of ancient Rome]? . . . Does the attitude of that Albany mob bespeak a way of life for many Americans? . . . If so, the bell tolls for all of us."

How would you answer *The Times*? Are human beings naturally cruel? Do we simply not feel any tie to a stranger? Do we secretly enjoy the drama of violence so long as we are not its victims? If your answers are yes, then what is *human* about us? Are we mere beasts of the jungle? If your answers are no, how can you explain the apathy of human beings who can sit by the blood of their neighbors and be unwilling to get involved?

These are not easy questions. They aren't easy now, and they weren't easy thousands of years ago when the prophets of Israel first began to deal with them. Five hundred years before the prophets, in the time of Moses, those who struggled with these issues and who wrote the earlier sections of the Bible knew that tough questions produce even tougher answers. They knew from their experience that people had to be not only individually responsible, willing to take risks for themselves, but also for the society in which they lived. They said it this way:

> If, however, there is a needy person among you, one of your kinsmen in any of your settlements in the land that the Lord your God is giving you, do not harden your heart and shut your hand against your needy kinsman. Rather, you must open your hand and lend him sufficient for whatever he needs.
>
> Deut. 15:7–8

You have heard the same thought expressed even more dramatically: "You shall love your neighbor as yourself." And who is your neighbor? Is it your friend next door with whom you walk to school? Yes. Is it your kindred Jews? Yes. But it is also the person you don't know who gets mugged on the school stairway; the black, Italian, or member of another minority who you don't know but who you hear being insulted. It is the family living in a part of town you never visit that, for historic reasons you had nothing to do with, is today undereducated, discriminated against, out of a job, living a miserable existence on welfare. Your neighbor is also a child across the sea, dying of starvation.

In other words, your neighbor is also the stranger at your gate, the widow, the orphan, the gentile. All of us are responsible, not only for ourselves but for just treatment of others as well. The prophets condemned people who looked out only for themselves and took no responsibility for the suffering of others. "Do not profit by the blood of your neighbor " (Lev. 19:16). "He who can protest, and does not, he incurs his punishment" (Sabbath 54b and Avodah 18a).

So far we have spoken mostly about what human beings are supposed to do. But what about God in all this? Doesn't God play a role? After all, God created all of us. If so, then surely God must have known what was being put into us. Why are we even made with a desire to deny or slander our fellow human beings? And so the last question we should ask is: *Is God really just?*

The question haunts Jewish history down to our own time. What was the dread crime which six million Jews committed which can explain the Nazi holocaust? Was each of them guilty of breaking God's law? That is absurd. Millions of devout, God-fearing, righteous people were led to the crematoria for only one crime: the crime of being *Jewish!* Where was God? There are some Jewish thinkers who, having grappled with this terrible question, concluded that God, too, died in the concentration camps. After Auschwitz, they say, one can no longer in conscience talk about a living

God. Elie Wiesel, the eloquent writer of the Holocaust, charges that God was silent to the people's cries. Others say that God cannot be blamed for this barbarity—*people* chose to do it, not God; and God gave us the freedom to do good or evil. Still others say the six million had to die to bring forth the miracle of Israel reborn. They argue that without the slaughter of the Nazi nightmare, there could never have been an Israel, sprung from the ashes and the blood in 1948. As individuals and groups, we often suffer because of the sins of others, just as we frequently benefit from their virtues, their talents, their courage.

The Holocaust came about because of the sins of society at large, from a lack of individual responsibility on the part of so many. As a result, many innocent, decent people suffered, and millions died.

What do you think? How do you explain the Holocaust? Were the Jews being punished? For what? And if so, wasn't this a breaking of the promise God made to Abraham and of the assurance of Ezekiel? Has the God who once spoke to the people retired into the silent mists of history? Or are we really seeking to blame God for the savagery of human beings?

Obviously, Jews are not the only people who have had to cry out in anguish against the injustice that has been visited upon them as a group. Were all the people of Hiroshima and Nagasaki bad people who deserved the catastrophe of nuclear death rained down upon them in World War II? Were the babies evil? Were they being punished for the evildoing of their parents and their rulers? Was that just? Or what about the millions of Cambodians destroyed by their own bloody Communist rulers? Or the Israelis killed in their settlements by guerrilla rockets? Or the Lebanese children bombed by Israel in reprisal against terrorism? What religious principle justifies these horrors? Were they punished for their own sins, or for the sins of their enemies? Can we make sense of these events? Does God know about them? Could it be that, through the Jewish people, God merely gave the world the game plan of how we should treat our fellow human beings and then left the field for us to play the game as we chose, good or bad, human or barbaric?

Whatever the role of God today, whether active or passive, *each of us is still responsible.* We are not all guilty, but we are all responsible. If people are starving in our land, or anywhere, *we* are responsible to prevent it. If native Indians are still exploited and oppressed in America, *we* are responsible because America is doing the oppressing. What Judaism demands is action to rectify wrongs. "You are the man," said Nathan. The enemy is "us"!

That is the message of the prophets—and of our tortured history: *each person,* if he or she is to be worthy of God and of humanity, must be responsible for conduct and for the lifting of pain and misery afflicting any other human being in the world.

BACK TO FRANK AND NAT

We've come a long way from Frank and Nat's problems. In the light of our rather global discussion, their questions might no longer seem so important. But they are important, for Frank and Nat are a small world in and of themselves— a microcosm. What they feel and how they react will determine the answers to the larger questions we have posed throughout this chapter. So, what should Frank and Nat do? We'll tell you what we think, and you think through your own reactions.

Frank should make certain he reports to the school authorities every instance of extortion and theft he sees or experiences. He should insist that the school authorities, students, and faculty punish every individual guilty of such outrageous behavior. And he should stop worrying about whether or not his schoolmates like or don't like him for what he does. There are values much more important than popularity. It takes courage to recognize that and to act on that recognition. The alternatives are far worse than being ridiculed and shunned by schoolmates who have neither the insight nor the intelligence to see that unless they too act honestly, they will eventually suffer even greater abuse and violations. Silence in the face of blackmail and extortion only emboldens the evildoer.

As for Nat, we think that while he ought to be respectful of his grandfather, understanding his pain and his hatred, Nat need not blindly follow the path of unforgiving hatred exhibited by his grandpa. He needs to overcome that hatred, recognizing, as we suspect he does, that a new generation and new conditions require new responses. If men and women are to perpetuate group prejudices eternally, there is no hope for humanity ever to aspire to the unity proclaimed by God's prophets.

XII

Intermarriage

STRICTLY speaking, Ezra was not a prophet. What, then, is he doing in this book? If he were alive and preaching today, many people would object to what he stood for. Yet he and his colleague, Nehemiah, are among Judaism's most respected historic personalities. In fact there are two books in the Bible which bear their names, and a third one, the Book of Ruth, was written sometime after their deaths to refute what they taught. Controversial? That's putting it mildly. In their day, they preached up a storm that is still raging today. The issue: intermarriage and the preservation of the Jewish family.

To understand Ezra and his message, one must first understand the history that moved him to preach it.

You remember that Babylon was invaded and conquered by the Persians in the year 539 B.C.E. The Persian leader, King Cyrus (550–530 B.C.E.), issued the famous "Edict of Liberation" shortly after the conquest. The document opened the doors for those Jews living in Babylon who wished to return to Palestine. It is interesting to see the difference between the way Cyrus understood what he did and the way Jews, living and writing at the time, interpreted the edict. It is a classic example of the way in which people interpret events to suit their own religious needs. Cyrus's account is found on the famous Cyrus Cylinder, a clay barrel found in Babylonia, and which describes his conquest of the Babylonians:

I returned to (these) sacred cities on the other side of the Tigres, the sanctuaries of which have been in ruins for a long time, the images which (used) to live therein and established for them permanent sanctuaries. I (also) gathered all their (former) inhabitants and returned (to them) their habitations.

That action is seen differently by Jewish commentators:

In the first year of Cyrus king of Persia, that the word of the Lord by the mouth of Jeremiah might be accomplished, the Lord stirred up the spirit of Cyrus king of Persia, that he made a proclamation throughout all his kingdom, and put it also in writing, saying: Thus says Cyrus king of Persia: All the kingdoms of the earth has the Lord, the God of heaven, given me; and He has charged me to build Him a house in Jerusalem, which is in Judah. Whosoever there is among you of all His people—his God be with him—let him go up to Jerusalem, which is in Judah, and build the house of the Lord, the God of Israel, He is the God who is in Jerusalem. And whosoever is left, in any place where he sojourns, let the men of his place help him with silver, and with gold, and with goods, and with beasts, beside the freewill offering for the house of God which is in Jerusalem.

Ezra 1:1–4

In the first year of Cyrus the king, Cyrus the king made a decree: Concerning the house of God at Jerusalem, let the house be built, the place where they offer sacrifices, and let the foundations thereof be strongly laid; the height thereof threescore cubits, and the breadth thereof threescore cubits; with three rows of great stones, and a row of new timber, and let the expenses be given out of the king's house; and also let the gold and silver vessels of the house of God, which Nebuchadnezzar took forth out of the Temple which is at Jerusalem, and brought unto Babylon, be restored, and brought back to the Temple which is at Jerusalem, every one to its place, and you shalt put them in the house of God.

Ezra 6:3–5

According to Ezra, it was God's will that the people be allowed to return to Palestine. It was God who "stirred up the spirit of Cyrus" even as it was God who gave Cyrus the strength to conquer "all the kingdoms of the earth." Which of the two versions is right? Are both of them? Do these varying interpretations help you better understand how history is written and what is meant by the suggestion that the writers of the Bible had a purpose to their writing?

The person (or persons) who wrote the biblical account of this bit of postexilic history is known as the Chronicler. He wrote much of what is found in 1 and 2 Chronicles in the Bible, as well as Ezra and Nehemiah, which were originally combined into one book. (They were divided into two separate books in the fourth century of the Common Era. This was done by a Christian Bible translator, Jerome, who produced a Latin translation. Known as the Vulgate, this is now the official translation of the Roman Catholic Church.)

The Chronicler's viewpoint was a priestly one. He reinterpreted Israelite history to show his conviction that the people of Israel were called by God to be a worshipping community—"a kingdom of priests and a holy people," a people whose whole life was to show divine service. The people's religious life was to center in the Temple in Jerusalem.

The facts of this postexilic period are a bit complicated. In the year 538 B.C.E., Cyrus issued his edict. He then appointed Sheshbazzar, the son of Jehoiachin, the exiled Judean king, to oversee the return. In effect, Cyrus handed over the leadership of the Jews to a prince of the Davidic line. Sheshbazzar was soon succeeded by Zerubbabel, also a descendant of the Jewish king, who led a small group of Jews back from Babylonia to Jerusalem. It was not a mass exodus as the Books of Ezra and Nehemiah understandably try to make us believe (see Neh. 7). Some scholars think that no more than 1,500 people made the long and hazardous journey. The famous Jewish historian, Josephus, was probably quite correct when he wrote that many in Babylon were reluctant to leave their possessions (see *Antiquities of the Jews* XII, 3) and uproot their lives in Babylonia.

Among the first acts of this new community was the building of a small altar in Jerusalem, on the site of the ruined Temple. They installed the Levites as administrators of the temple cult, and they laid the foundations for a new temple. For the next eight years, the effort was constantly interrupted by a group of people, who lived in the northern part of Palestine (known as the Samaritans). Their center was, and still is, Nablus-Schechem. It is today the heart of that area known as the West Bank. The Samaritans were Jews who were not exiled to Babylonia. Being northerners, they had been conquered much earlier by the Assyrians (721 B.C.E.) and, in a real sense, had been separated, and separated themselves, from the main body of the surviving Jewish community. While they clung to the Torah laws as they interpreted them, they did not feel bound to the Jerusalem Temple, so that its destruction by the Babylonians did not shatter their religious life. Many intermarried with foreign husbands and wives, and assimilated with the larger non-Jewish community in Israel. Still, the Samaritans considered themselves true Jews, faithful to the Mosaic tradition, interested in seeing the Jerusalem Temple restored as a religious, but not as a national, center.

When Zerubbabel brought the people back, the Samaritans at first offered to assist in the reconstruction of the sanctuary. Their offer was rejected. They withdrew and built a rival Samaritan temple on Mt. Gerizim overlooking Shechem. Their harassment of the small community halted the work of rebuilding. It was not resumed until the year 520 B.C.E. and was not completed for five years. The Temple they built was a small, very modest structure, in no way comparable to the majestic building put up by Solomon. Yet, it served as the center of Israel's life in this period. People believed that God had again taken up residence among the people Israel. Two minor prophets, Haggai and Zechariah, whose brief books we find in the Hebrew Bible, encouraged the people to complete the Temple during this period and inspired them with dreams of restored national glory. They went so far as to suggest that Zerubbabel was the personification of the long-awaited national messiah—the redeemer of Israel (see Zech. 6:12–13).

For the next three-quarters of a century, Israel was ruled by Persian governors sent by the powerful Persian kings. It was not an easy time for the small community of returnees. They were threatened constantly by outside neighboring peoples and weakened from within by poverty, discontent, and religious apathy. To make matters worse, many succumbed to the pressures of the larger non-Jewish culture in which they found themselves. Intermarriage was so widespread that it became a topic for prophetic condemnation (Mal. 2:11–12).

Nehemiah was a cupbearer to the Persian King Artaxerxes I (465–424 B.C.E.), in the court at Susa, the Persian winter capital. He had heard shocking reports of the dismal conditions in Jerusalem. He persuaded the king to give him the authority of a governor and to send him to Jerusalem to rebuild the city's defenses. The first four chapters of the biblical book that bears his name detail these events. The city's walls were rebuilt in fifty-two days. But Nehemiah was more than an engineer-governor. He was a man with strong ideas of how to reform the inner life of the people. Since he wanted to eliminate the effect of the Samaritans, the Ammonites living in Transjordan, and the Edomites to the south of Jerusalem, Nehemiah introduced and enforced a strict policy of nonfraternization with these surrounding people. He believed that membership in the Jewish community was determined by birth; that is, by whether or not your mother and grandmother were Jewish. To preserve the purity of the Jewish people, he strictly prohibited intermarriage.

You shall not give your daughters to their sons, or take their daughters for your sons or for yourselves.

Neh. 13:25

This was not the first condemnation of intermarriage. Marriage with any person outside the Israelite community had always been condemned and forbidden (see Deut. 7:3 and Gen. 28:2) from the earliest beginnings of Jewish history. The people of Israel have sought to preserve their ethnic identity by prohibiting intermarriage. While there are no references in prophetic literature specifically condemning intermarriage, the prophets were consistently opposed to any action which would threaten the cohesiveness or integrity of the group.

Some years after Nehemiah's first appearance in Jerusalem (about 428 B.C.E.), a priest named Ezra received permission to bring a caravan of Jewish exiles from Babylon to Palestine. Ezra was a priest and a scribe skilled in the laws of Moses. But he was more; he, too, was a religious reformer filled with the kind of zeal that so often characterizes such personalities.

We are told that Ezra carried with him from Babylon a copy of "the book of the law of Moses." One day he read this completely to the people in a public square in Jerusalem. The climax of the event came when the people confessed their sins, promised to separate themselves from all foreigners, and solemnly renewed the covenant (see Ezra 10:3). This covenant document was officially signed by the Jewish leaders, and the rest of the people gave their assent. The entire experience reminds one very strongly of the much earlier covenant ceremony of Josiah (2 Kings 23:1–3).

While no one knows the exact contents of this "book of the law of Moses" that Ezra read to the people, it is probable that whatever he read contained elements of the priestly legislation, sections of the book of Deuteronomy, and the Torah as edited by the priests during the Babylonian exile. But whatever else he may have read to the people on that day, it is clear that he demanded not only that the people no longer intermarry, but also that they divorce their non-Jewish wives!

> Separate yourselves from the peoples of the land and from the foreign wives.
>
> Ezra 10:11

He justified his demand by invoking the authority of Deuteronomic law. See Ezra 9:10–14, especially verse 14:

> Shall we break thy commandments again and intermarry with the peoples who practice these abominations?

The demands of Nehemiah and Ezra must have caused terrible domestic and family tragedies. Imagine a husband and wife forced to separate. Imagine the misery children must have gone through. It is bad enough for children to be separated from their fathers or mothers after a divorce where the couple voluntarily decide they can no longer live with one another; but consider the pain caused to all when, in the name of God or religion, families are forced apart.

Nevertheless, Jews of the time responded to the priest's demands. While we are told that the people agreed to and acted on Ezra's demands, putting away all foreign wives (Ezra 10:16), we know that there was also a negative response. And that, too, is found in the Bible. The narrow exclusiveness of Nehemiah and Ezra was protested in the form of the charming story of Ruth. The writer of that book placed the story in the rural setting of ancient Israel, during the time of the tribal confederacy before David unified the country. Ruth, a Moabite woman, married Boaz, a Hebrew. Their son, Obed, became the father of Jesse, the father of David, Israel's greatest king (Ruth 4:17). In other words, the author wanted to show that God's greatest favor was bestowed upon Israel through an intermarriage—the very thing that Nehemiah and Ezra frowned upon. The Book of Ruth is a very attractive piece of propaganda against the notion that one's position within the Jewish people depended solely upon purity of blood or correctness of genealogy. Judaism was intrigued by this idea. It became the practice to read the Book of Ruth at Shavuot, the holiday commemorating the giving of the Ten Commandments, to show that those laws were for all people, not just Jews.

The difference in the two historical situations cannot be overlooked. Ezra was struggling to preserve the survival of the Jewish people at a time when the widespread practice of intermarriage seemed to threaten that survival. The situation described in the Book of Ruth is entirely different. This is the case of an individual who converts to Judaism and thus poses no threat at all to the survival of the Jews.

Do you think Nehemiah and Ezra were right in what they did? Before you answer, remember that the goal of these two zealots was more than an effort to maintain Jewish purity. It was fundamentally a struggle to preserve the identity of the Jewish people and the uniqueness of Israel's faith in the face of the tremendous cultural pressures at work on them during the Persian period. Nehemiah had correctly reminded the people of the folly of Solomon's universalism. Solomon had permitted his foreign wives to introduce into the Temple liturgy the worship of their foreign gods. This practice eventually destroyed the unified kingdom and so weakened the Jewish state that it broke apart after Solomon's death. That fact, perhaps more than any other, opened the people to attacks from outside and eventually to the loss of the entire northern kingdom to Assyria.

The question we have asked is not altogether an academic one, nor have we given you all this ancient history just as a recitation of events that happened 2,400 years ago with no application to modern times. On the contrary, the same debate is now raging in the American Jewish community. There are some, perhaps many, who view the current trend toward intermarriage and threat of assimilation with the same alarm as did Nehemiah and Ezra. It affects and will affect you profoundly. If present statistics apply to you, four out of ten of you and your friends will marry non-Jews. Nearly 50 percent of you will not join a congregation when you are adults or give your children any formal Jewish education. What does that imply for the future of Judaism in America?

INTERMARRIAGE AND THE FAMILY

The Jewish family is in trouble today. There are ample danger signals. Jews are producing fewer children than before. The average number of children produced by Catholic parents in the United States is 2.8 per family, 2.3 for Protestants, and 2.1 for Jews. Some Jews make a kind of sick joke of this statistic when they say that Jews are the best practitioners of birth control and Z.P.G. (Zero Population Growth) in the world. Jokes aside, we are not growing in numbers, and we are declining as a percentage of the total population. There are some in the Jewish community who seriously urge Jewish couples to have more children to offset this downward trend, and they base their opposition to birth control, family planning, and abortion on the fact of a declining Jewish population. They say that a declining Jewish birth rate is a posthumous victory for Hitler. What do they mean?

There are also those who dismiss this fear. They say that more does not mean better. A larger *quantity* of Jews in America or the world will not mean a finer *quality* of Jews. Jewish birth does not guarantee that one will remain Jewish or identify with the Jewish people. Numbers do not insure Judaism. There are more Jews in America (5.7 million) than there are either Episcopalians (3 million) or Presbyterians (2.8 million), and certainly more Jews than there are Quakers (250,000). Yet these Christian groups make an impact, and few of these groups so worry about their survival that they advocate more births, nor do they take positions in opposition to population limitations because of their own small numbers. Conversely, these groups argue strongly for measures to limit world population and to control family size because they see a larger, more serious problem of an overly populated world which this earth cannot sustain. They are concerned about world hunger, disease, and high rates of infant mortality, situations which exist because there are too many people in the world.

How do you feel about the suggestion that Jewish parents be encouraged to have more children? Can you defend that proposition while, at the same time, urging programs of population control for the rest of the world? Do you believe that the future health of Judaism and the Jewish people depends on larger Jewish families?

Those who worry about the deterioration of the Jewish family also point to the rising divorce rate among Jews. Today, one out of every two marriages in America ends in divorce. The rate among Jews may be slightly lower but it, too, is rising rapidly. It is harder to maintain a feeling of family where mothers and fathers live apart, in different locations. It is not impossible, however, especially if one of the partners remarries and the children live with a natural parent and a stepparent. Moreover, it is possible for husbands and wives to live apart from one another, even though they may share a common physical space. Conventional wisdom urged couples with children to stay together "for the sake of the children," even when their personal relationship had deteriorated to a point where the love that initially brought them together had either evaporated or turned to hate. That kind of advice is not given so often today. Forcing two people who are incompatible to remain together can be even more injurious to them, and to the health and welfare of the children involved, than is separation and divorce. The writer of the Book of Proverbs taught an important lesson in the verse:

> Better is a dry morsel with quiet
> than a house full of feasting with strife.
>
> Prov. 17:1

No one does, or should, take lightly the breakup of a marriage—the hurts and pains are too many and too serious. Certainly Judaism didn't. The Talmud put it this way:

> He who puts away the wife of his youth, for him God's very altar weeps.
>
> Sanhedrin 22a

But Judaism, unlike some other religions, does not prohibit divorce. "It recognizes that even more tragic than the separation of husband and wife is their living a life of pretense and deceit" (*My Beloved Is Mine*, Rabbi Roland B. Gittelsohn, UAHC, 1969, p. 202).

Contrary to what some may think, the Bible does allow for divorce:

> A man takes a wife and possesses her. She fails to please him because he finds something obnoxious about her, and he writes her a bill of divorcement, hands it to her, and sends her away from his house.
>
> Deut. 24:1

While lower birth and growing divorce rates among Jews are considered by some experts as important reasons for the decline in the strength of the Jewish family, the force still considered the number one enemy of the Jewish family is intermarriage. Like Ezra and Nehemiah, many Jews today see their survival in terms of self-segregation, staying away from too intimate a contact with non-Jews and the non-Jewish culture. They argue that, because we Jews are a shrinking minority in a majority culture, the only way to avoid being overwhelmed by that culture is to avoid intermarriage in every possible way. The marriage of a Jew to a non-Jew, they feel, brings the culture of the non-Jewish world into the Jewish home in a most intimate and corrupting way. The Hebrew prophets shared this attitude. Every time a Jewish king married a foreign woman, he was

severely condemned by a prophet. The most famous confrontation between a king and a prophet over this issue
occurred when Elijah rebuked Ahab, king of the northern
tribes of Israel, for marrying Jezebel, the daughter of a king
of Sidon (a country to the north of Israel), and for allowing
her to introduce the worship of her god Baal into the royal
court. Elijah challenged the king to prove the power of Baal
against the power of God. Two altars were built on Mount
Carmel near the modern city of Haifa and sacrifices were
offered up, first by the prophets of Baal, and then by Elijah.
The results were devastating, and the affair ended up with
the slaughter of 950 of Jezebel's false prophets. (This dramatic incident is found in 1 Kings, chapter 18.)

The problem of intermarriage has not disappeared.
Today, the arguments about intermarriage are growing
even more heated. Is intermarriage a serious threat to the
Jewish family and to our survival as Jews? Is self-segregation
good? Is it possible in our modern culture? America is seeking to destroy racial ghettos. Are they to be replaced by
religious ones? If separate but equal is bad, is "separate but
better" good?

Albert Vorspan's book, *Jewish Values and Social Crisis*,
quotes the following letter from a Jewish girl in Dayton,
Ohio, who was soon to be married to a non-Jewish boy. She
puts the issues before us in passionate and challenging
terms:

> Wake up, you Dayton Jewish Community! Quit making a
> mockery of interfaith dating. You are the ones who insist
> on our lack of prejudice; you are the ones who arrange the
> interfaith meetings, the evening get-togethers among Jew-
> ish and gentile boys and girls. For these things, you are
> gung ho!
>
> But just let one of your sons or daughters even mention
> that they might want to go out with someone of another
> faith, and POW! It's total disaster. Don't deny it! Don't
> claim that you've never been guilty! I have known too

many teen-agers who have been sneaking out behind your backs with fellows and girls of other faiths for the majority of their dating years because YOU made it taboo. What are you afraid of? Are you worried that your son or daughter will marry a non-Jew? Is interfaith marriage necessarily wrong?

I am involved in an interfaith relationship which will consummate shortly in marriage. I have a friend who is also dating a gentile boy and plans to marry him. We have both examined our feelings thoroughly. We have both been willing to discuss our relationships with our parents.

Isn't it interesting that our family rabbi, who had known us for years, was somewhat unwilling to really talk about the problem? He merely said that the relationship was "wrong." He was too busy and too unconcerned to really probe the situation.

And yet, the priest, while not condoning the relationship, at least sat and talked about the situation for a longer period of time, at least probed the motives and tried to understand.

Fortunately, my parents have never discouraged my specific relationship. We have discussed all aspects of the problem, pros and cons. We have discussed the ultimate conflicts which might arise as a result of a mixed marriage.

My parents believe that I have an intelligent mind of my own and that I am capable of reasoning out the situation. They have always respected this boy FOR WHAT HE IS.

I know there will be problems. I don't deny that fact. But they won't necessarily be ones of religious nature. I'm tired of your clichés like "marriage has enough problems of its own."

Isn't marriage better when two people have very much in common, when they are truly in love with one another, when they hold the same basic beliefs about life? How much better than the marriage where the partners are of the same religion and were married because "mamma approved of a nice Jewish boy"?

Will I convert? Will he convert? How will we rear our children? These are questions which we are continuing to probe. We are two intelligent human beings who are bound and determined to go into a marriage relationship with our eyes wide open. Our decisions will be our own.

You and your children, given similar circumstances, might reach other decisions. You are entitled to reach these decisions as individuals.

But, parents, please remember this: we who are involved in interfaith relationships do not intend to give up our Jewish heritage. If you, our families, really want us to have good lives and happy marriages, then don't attempt to restrict our acquaintances by their religious beliefs. You are being petty. There are a great many good and worthwhile people in this world, and each of us should have the chance to seek out our best mate—regardless of religious faith.

Let's look at some of the statistics.

The rate of intermarriage (the marriage of a Jew to a person who was not Jewish at the time the couple first met) has risen from 13 percent in 1960 to 37 percent by 1970, and some say that today it is even as high as 50 or 60 percent. Do you think your marrying a non-Jew might weaken your ties or commitment to maintaining a Jewish family? If not, why not? If so, why?

Why has intermarriage increased so dramatically? Sociologists claim that one of the reasons is the increasing opportunity for American Jews to integrate into the larger society. This leads to widespread social mixing where the influence of the prevailing culture is stronger than traditional Jewish values. For example, it may be more common for Jews to enjoy some social event on a Friday evening than it is for them together, as a family, to observe and enjoy the Shabbat, at home and temple. In a "closed" Jewish community, it would be impossible for Jews to participate in some secular social event. In an open society, there is nothing to prevent them from doing so. Somehow being Jewish just doesn't seem as important as it once did.

A second reason for the increase in intermarriage may be the acceptance of intermarriage as a normal activity. The more it happens, the more normal it becomes. And it is increasingly considered normal, since it happens more frequently. This is what is known as a *Catch 22* situation. Intermarriage is no longer seen as an act of rebellion against being Jewish or as a conscious effort to assimilate, to lose or give up one's identity as a Jew. Many young Jews who intermarry consider intermarriage and retaining their Jewish identity consistent with each other. If this is the case, then what does being Jewish mean?

It is natural to wonder about the Jewish education or Jewish exposure of the children of an intermarriage. A recent sampling in Boston (reported by Leonard J. Fein) showed that only 28 percent of the intermarried (without conversion of the non-Jewish partner to Judaism) were raising their children as Jews (compared with 91 percent, where there was conversion to Judaism). Where the wife was Jewish, 98.4 percent of the children of the intermarriage were raised as Jewish. The woman, it seems, tends to retain her religious identity and to determine the religious orientation of her children. In cases where only the husband is Jewish, the percentage of children raised as Jews dropped to 63.3 percent. In other words, the less intermarriage, the more likely it is that the children will be raised as Jews.

There is a definite and direct relationship between a Jew's indifference to his or her Jewishness and the likelihood that such a person may marry a non-Jew. Where the husband was Jewish, the likelihood of intermarriage was 55.1 percent among those whose upbringing was characterized as "uncertain" (whether Jewish or not Jewish), 26.7 percent if upbringing was "not at all Jewish," 13.0 percent if "somewhat Jewish," but only 2.5 percent if "strongly Jewish."

Rabbis who officiate at marriages between a Jew and a non-Jew defend their actions on a number of grounds. They say that the Jewish community should face reality. Jews should accept the fact that the rate of intermarriage is increasing and attempt to save for Judaism as many of these couples as possible by not rejecting them. They maintain that coming to a rabbi and asking him or her to officiate is a positive step on the couple's part, an indication of their desire to keep a relationship in and with the Jewish community. To refuse them this rabbinical service is to risk turning them off and turning them away from Judaism for the future. They further argue that one cannot preach the universalism as found in the Book of Ruth while practicing the particularism of Ezra. To do so is hypocritical.

One Reform rabbi who does officiate at intermarriages put it this way. "Among my tasks as a rabbi are to preserve Judaism, to represent the Jewish community vertically in history and horizontally in the present, and to serve God through serving His children. Intermarriage is a fact of life. I seek to use the opportunity provided for me by those who come to me, a rabbi, when contemplating marriage to find a way of keeping them related to the Jewish community and the Jewish tradition" (Rabbi Michael Robinson, Intermarriage Seminar, 1972, UAHC).

A rabbi who refuses to officiate at mixed marriages declares: "The general Jewish public believes that just as salt is used to kosher meat a rabbi can be used to make kosher out of *treife*. I was taught by my teachers at HUC that the irreducible minimum for a *Jewish* wedding is that both parties be Jewish." This rabbi assailed the notion that such couples would be saved for Judaism and he cited a colleague who, having performed mixed marriages for years, did a follow-up study on the Jewishness of such couples. The results so disillusioned the rabbi that he abandoned his practice of officiating at such marriages.

The number of Reform rabbis who officiate at intermarriages is still small, but it is growing. No Orthodox or Conservative rabbi can or will officiate. They are prohibited from doing so by Jewish religious law, called *Halachah,* to which the Orthodox strictly adhere and to which all Conservative rabbis claim to be loyal. The Reform rabbinate as an institution maintains its formal opposition to such practice. In 1973, the Central Conference of American Rabbis adopted the following resolution:

> The Central Conference of American Rabbis, recalling its stand adopted in 1909 that "mixed marriage is contrary to the Jewish tradition and should be discouraged," now declares its opposition to participation by its members in any ceremony which solemnizes a mixed marriage.
>
> The Central Conference of American Rabbis recognizes that historically its members have held and continue to hold divergent interpretations of Jewish tradition.
>
> In order to keep open every channel to Judaism and K'lal Yisrael for those who have already entered into mixed marriage, the CCAR calls upon its members:
> 1. to assist fully in educating children of such mixed marriages as Jews;
> 2. to provide the opportunity for conversion of the non-Jewish spouse; and
> 3. to encourage a creative and consistent cultivation of involvement in the Jewish community and the synagogue.

It may be interesting to see how Jewish teenagers view this problem of intermarriage. In the early seventies, Jewish teenagers in New Orleans were asked about it. Thirty percent of the young people who came from Reform backgrounds saw intermarriage as likely to lead to problems within the family. But 70 percent said people should marry whom they love without regard to religion. Only 35 percent of the non-Reform youngsters agreed with this. Three trends seem to stand out among these teenagers. A large majority reject intermarriage, but see it as undesirable rather than calami-

tous; romantic love overrides a potential spouse's non-Jew-
ishness. Girls are more hesitant about intermarriage. (Fewer
Jewish females marry non-Jewish males than Jewish males
marry non-Jewish females.) And while parental attitude
plays an inhibiting role, the unclear and vacillating feelings
many parents have toward their own Judaism and toward
intermarriage, together with the young people's belief that
all will eventually be forgiven, probably result in a dilution
of the negative effect such disapproval has on the young
person's final decision.

It seems that when the value of romantic love collides
with the values of Jewish identity or preserving a Jewish
home, frequently the former wins over the latter. If this is
true, can the Jewish people survive as a group in a totally
free and open society? Those who answer yes point to the
high rate of conversion to Judaism by those who do intermarry. The decline in anti-Semitism and the acceptance of
the Jew as a part of the pluralism of America seem to have
taken the shame out of conversion to Judaism. Thus, many
who fall in love with and seek to marry Jews become Jews
through conversion with an ease and openness that did not
previously exist in this country. It is interesting to note that
in a 1972 survey, nearly half (45.6 percent of the non-Jewish
wives and 43.5 percent of the non-Jewish husbands) of the
initially non-Jewish spouses answered yes when asked, "Are
you Jewish now?"—despite the fact that only 26.7 percent
of the initially non-Jewish wives and only 2.5 percent of the
initially non-Jewish husbands had converted. How do you
think Ezra and Nehemiah would have felt about that statistic? Would they have accepted into the Jewish community
unconverted non-Jews who claimed to be Jewish and who,
as in the Book of Ruth, wished to cast their lot with the
Jewish people? Ruth, you will remember, was the one who
said no to her Jewish mother-in-law, Naomi, after the death
of Ruth's husband, when Naomi urged her daughter-in-law
to return to Moab, the land from which she came:

Entreat me not to leave you and to return from following
you for where you go, I will go; and where you lodge, I will
lodge; your people shall be my people and your God my
God; where you die, I will die, and there will I be buried.

Ruth 1:16–17

WHAT ABOUT INTERDATING?

We know that most young people reading this book are not
much concerned about marriage. It probably seems to be
something that is light years away, and thinking about the
problems of a possible intermarriage might very well seem
to be something altogether unreal. No doubt you have given
thought to whether or not to go out with a non-Jewish boy
or girl. Will interdating lead to intermarriage? In the early
teenage years, probably not. But the older you become, the
closer you get to marriageable age, the more realistic the
question becomes—and the more difficult the answer.

It is probably true that the more one interdates the
more one increases the possibility that he or she will fall in
love and possibly establish a permanent relationship with
the person being dated. It takes a person very strongly committed to his or her faith and tradition to be able to distinguish a non-Jewish date from a possible mate or life partner.
It isn't easy to realize that good dates may not necessarily
make good mates. A mate is someone with whom one ought
to have as much in common as possible. One wise man once
said that the only unlikes that should mate are those unlike
in sex, but alike in most other respects. Religious and cultural backgrounds are an important part of what shapes a
person's attitudes, behavior, eating habits, even attitudes
toward sex. And since marriage at its best is full of hazards
and requires the most delicate adjustments, it is better not
to add the extra hurdle of religious and ethnic difference to
the obstacles already in the path of a successful marriage.

Young people often say: "But religion means little to us,

why should we let it separate us?" Superficially, that argument sounds persuasive. It is true that some people can get along with no religion. However, when a non-Jew marries someone Jewish, the association is with more than religion. The word "Jew," like the word "Italian," or "French," embraces a world of attitudes, feelings, history, culture, language, and customs. The same is true for "Christian." There are psychological differences which are enormously powerful even though they may not appear at first, covered as they are by the waves of romantic love. But many a marriage has foundered on those differences after the passion has ebbed and the problems of daily living in marriage emerge. Tragic experiences sometime confront couples who marry without facing, in advance, the implications of the differences in culture and belief. Those awkward differences can become painful when children arrive and decisions have to be reached over whether to have the child baptized, or given a name in the synagogue, or circumcised in a *Berit Milah,* or given a religious education. A religiously united home is far more likely to survive than one religiously and culturally divided. Studies indicate that children raised in home atmospheres that are neither Jewish nor Gentile are at a disadvantage.

By the time they reach college, many of these children are embittered against their parents for this lack of preparation. Psychological tests show that even while in high school, many of the children of these religiously indifferent homes have greater uncertainty about their own moral worth and identity and are more prone to feelings of self-rejection than children who come from either Jewish or Christian homes. They do not know on what ground they stand.

There seems to be more to this notion of Jewish peoplehood than meets the eye. It is worth thinking about even as you contemplate interdating, which admittedly may be a long, long way from getting married.

Obviously, Ezra and Nehemiah had no knowledge of these sociological and psychological studies. Those words were not even a part of their vocabulary. But, they did have feelings based on their observations, their experiences, and their commitment to a God who demanded exclusivity. What they called for must have appeared as cruel and as hard then as it did to you when you first read about their message at the beginning of this chapter. But now, having studied some of the evidence and the statistics, do they still seem to be cruel and unreasonable? Your answers to these questions may very well shape the future of your lives, both maritally and Jewishly, and will certainly affect the future of the Jewish people.

XIII

Life

MANY times during the writing of this book we have asked, "If the prophets were alive today, what would they say about . . . ?" Given the enormous sweep of their vision, their capacity to rise up in times of social crisis and address that crisis with sharp, often stinging truth, it is hard to imagine that they would not have something very important to say about any number of the difficult situations which modern life forces upon us. Life may have been complicated in their days; it is far more complicated today. They did not know as much about the physical nature of the universe as we do. Neither were they able to manipulate life and death as humankind can now. No one then could press a button and destroy the world. No one in their day could predetermine the sex of an unborn child. No one could terminate a pregnancy with very little risk to the mother. And no one could create human life in a laboratory. No one could artificially prolong life to such a degree and in such a way that there was a real argument over when a person was actually or legally dead. No prophet had any knowledge of DNA, cloning, or the genetic structure of humanity which enabled them to affect how a person would grow or what a person might look like or think.

For good or ill, all these possibilities are available to us today. These capacities impose upon modern society ethical dilemmas about which the prophets did not even dream. In those days, nations went to war and destroyed a tiny percentage of the world's peoples, or for a brief time ruined some corner of the physical world; today in that same instant we can incinerate the entire world and wipe out almost its total population. In many ways we, today, deal with much more complex matters than did our prophetic forebears. Yet, perhaps things are not all that much more difficult or that different. Perhaps the same principles that governed decisions about life and death then still apply. Let's see.

CAPITAL PUNISHMENT

Few would quarrel with the statement that the prophets of Israel were passionate believers in life. Death was no virtue. The purpose of humanity was to live in order to proclaim the word of the Lord. Each prophet individually reiterated the theme that God takes no delight in destroying the evildoer. More than anything else, God only wanted humanity to turn away from its hurtful and destructive ways and return to God so that humanity might live and not die.

The prophet Ezekiel put it this way:

> Cast away all the transgressions by which you have offended, and get yourselves a new heart and a new spirit, that you may not die, O House of Israel. For it is not My desire that anyone shall die—declares the Lord God. Repent, therefore, and live!
>
> Ezek. 18:31–32 (see also Ezek. 33:11)

The prophet Jeremiah in his famous parable of the potter and the clay makes this sentiment strikingly clear:

> O House of Israel, can I not deal with you like this potter? —says the Lord. Just like clay in the hands of the potter, so are you in My hands, O House of Israel! At one moment I may decree that a nation or a kingdom shall be uprooted and pulled down and destroyed; but if that nation against which I made the decree turns back from its wickedness,

I change My mind concerning the punishment I planned to bring on it.

And now, say to the men of Judah and the inhabitants of Jerusalem: Thus said the Lord: I am devising disaster for you and laying plans against you. Turn back, each of you, from your wicked ways, and mend your ways and your actions!

Jer. 18:6–8; 11

The prophets pleaded with the people of Israel to act in such a way that they and their nation could stay alive. While their concern was more with the future of the people than it was with the survival of any individual, they were not insensitive to the value of the individual. Their concern for the future was with this world. The blessings were to be found on this earth, not in some other world to come. There was not anything particularly new in this emphasis. They built on the teachings of the biblical writers that preceded them. Perhaps the most famous expression of that biblical desire that people choose life here and now is found in the familiar passage

I call heaven and earth to witness against you this day: I have put before you life and death, blessing and curse. Choose life—if you and your offspring would live . . . .

Deut. 30:19

There is more to this wonderful passage than first meets the eye. Notice that life is equated with "blessing," while death is equated with "curse." Also notice the word "choose." It implies that people have freedom of will; that it is in their hands to choose how they will affirm (or defame) life. People are not controlled by God. They are free to choose what course of action they will take. This sentiment is expressed as early as the fourth chapter of Genesis, when God speaks to Cain:

Surely, if you do right,
There is uplift.
But if you do not do right
Sin is the demon at the door,
Whose urge is toward you,
Yet you can be his master.

Gen. 4:7

This idea of free will has never been lost in Judaism. A thousand years after these words were written, the rabbis of the first century wrote:

Everything is in the hands of God except the fear (read: awe) of God.

Megillah 25A, Berachot 33b

In other words, God, who may command everything, cannot force humanity to respect God. This notion that men and women are free to accept or reject the demands of Divinity is one of the most important ideas in all of Judaism. It affects everything we do or say or think about God, about one another. Nations, like individuals, also have that freedom of choice.

What would the prophets of Israel have said about the following?

In 1960, agents of the State of Israel's intelligence force found Adolf Eichmann living in a town in Argentina. In a melodramatic action, Israeli agents kidnapped Eichmann off the street of the town where he was living in hiding, secreted him on to a plane and flew him to Israel. There he was imprisoned, interrogated and then placed on trial. The charge: genocide—mass murder of Jews.

Adolf Eichmann was the Nazi most responsible for organizing the slaughter of six million Jews in Europe. He was the architect of what was known as the "Final Solution." When the war ended, Hitler's charred body was found in a bunker in Berlin, a suicide. Many leading Nazis were captured and punished at the Nuremberg Trials. A few were hanged, the rest sentenced to long prison terms. But Adolf Eichmann escaped.

The capture and trial of Eichmann raised a number of difficult questions. Some people said he should have been turned over to the West Germans. Some felt that Israel had acted illegally, and there were angry protests from all over the world. However, most people felt there was simple justice in the turn of events; that the greatest murderer of Jews in human history should be tried in a Jewish state by the very people he sought to wipe off the face of the earth.

The trial was thorough and agonizing. Dozens of survivors—some living in Israel, others brought from the four corners of the world—identified Eichmann as the man in charge of genocide.

Eichmann was found guilty, hanged, and cremated. His ashes were scattered in the Mediterranean Sea. It was the only instance of capital punishment in the history of Israel, for that country at its inception had eliminated the death penalty for all cases except the most heinous crime of mass murder. Even Arab terrorists who have brutally raided in Israel, killing innocent civilians, have not been subjected to the death penalty. Eichmann was the lone exception. A few Jews in Israel and throughout the world, who were against the death penalty on principle, even opposed it for Eichmann, arguing that the Jewish reverence for life should not have been compromised even in this most extreme instance. The majority, however, disagreed with this view. They cited the biblical command to take "an eye for an eye" to justify their position, even though that phrase had never been taken literally in Jewish tradition.

Which of these two views was right?

What would the prophets have said?

The Bible did provide for capital punishment. The death penalty was ordered for adulterers, those who practiced idolatry, and those who blaspheme (falsely use God's name when taking an oath). Even "a disloyal and defiant son" could be turned over to the elders of the city, who could order him stoned to death (Deut. 21:18–21). There are so many instances reported in the Bible of capital punishment being practiced (see Josh. 7:25, the stoning of Achan; 1 Kings 12:18, the stoning of Adoram; 1 Kings 21:13–15, the stoning of Naboth; Lev. 24:23, the stoning of the blasphemer) that it would be futile and false to suggest that the biblical tradition opposed this practice. However, it was not an act engaged in lightly. There was always a rigorous trial, at least two witnesses had to be found who could swear that they saw the accused commit the act for which he or she was being charged, and then the entire community participated in carrying out the death penalty. All the townspeople simultaneously stoned the guilty one.

The biblical phrase most commonly referred to by those who try to justify the continuing modern practice of capital punishment is the one found in Exodus 21:23–25. Here we read:

> . . . the penalty shall be life for life, eye for eye, tooth for tooth, hand for hand, foot for foot, burn for burn, wound for wound, bruise for bruise.

Almost identical language is found in a much earlier Babylonian legal code. It is called the Code of Hammurabi and was written around 2,500 B.C.E. by the great Babylonian king whose name this document bears:

> If a seignior has destroyed the eye of a member of the aristocracy they shall destroy his eye (as found in *Ancient Near Eastern Texts Relating to the Old Testament,* James B. Pritchard, Princeton University Press, Princeton, N.J., 1955, p. 175).

Actually much of the legal code of the ancient Hebrews found in the Bible was modeled on this earlier Babylonian code, though the Bible made many modifications on the

Code of Hammurabi. The biblical system was not nearly as
vindictive as the earlier code on which it was based. Later
the rabbis made even further modifications on this particular law of "an eye for an eye." Their abhorrence of capital
punishment led them to devise a system of monetary compensation for injury. By the time of the writing of the Mishnah (completed in 200 C.E.), the restrictions on capital punishment were so numerous (see Mishnah Sanhedrin 8:1–5)
that the effect was virtually to end the death penalty. In
Mishnah Makkot 1:10 a court is branded as "murderous" if it
imposes the death penalty as often as once in seven years
and, according to Rabbi Eleazar ben Azariah, once in sev-
enty years. Rabbi Tarphon and Rabbi Akiba opposed the
death penalty altogether, 1,900 years ago!

In light of this history and this tradition, were the Israelis justified in putting Eichmann to death? Did they have
alternatives to killing him? What else could they have done?
Were those Jews (and others) who opposed the death penalty for Eichmann asking too much of the Jewish people at
that time?

These questions raise some difficult issues for modern
society. Violence is on the increase everywhere. Terrorists
murder innocent bystanders. Athletes are slaughtered at
Olympic contests. In Europe, people are kidnapped not just
for ransom but for political purposes, by groups who wish to
recast society in their own image and who believe that their
ends justify any means. In the United States, buildings are
bombed by those who advocate freedom for their fellow
citizens in other countries. What should people and nations
do to protect themselves?

Society is beginning to give its answer. Because of the
rise of violence and terrorism throughout the world, because of the growing frequency with which crazy people
indiscriminately take life and law into their own hands,
Americans, at least, are beginning to protest against laws
which have eliminated the death penalty in a number of our
states. In the late 1970s there was a growing ground swell of

opposition to the Supreme Court decisions which severely limited the death penalty. In the fall of 1977, a poll was taken in New York City on the attitudes of its populace to the state's allowing capital punishment. An amazing 75 percent of the New Yorkers agreed that the death penalty should be restored. Seventy-eight percent of the Jews in New York City agreed with this view.

Is such an attitude an expression of justice being done, or is it only an expression of people's frustration and their desire to lash back in some vindictive way? Discuss the issue of capital punishment. Take a vote in your class on the issue of how the class feels about capital punishment. Is it ever punishment that fits the crime?

In light of all this, do you think that the prophet Hosea would have counselled the people of Israel to put Eichmann to death? Do you think that God would want the state to electrocute, hang, or gas the murderers of President Kennedy or his brother, Robert, or Martin Luther King, Jr.? How would you respond to the suggestion in Israel that terrorists be given the death penalty?

One last question before leaving this aspect of Judaism's attitude toward life: Do you believe it is possible for even the most hardened criminal to be rehabilitated? There are many complaints about the present conditions of American prisons. Many charge that putting people in prison today is only sending them to a graduate school for crime. There is much truth to this accusation. Our prisons are overcrowded and brutalizing places with little or no real opportunities for inmates to be truly rehabilitated. But is the solution to this situation to reduce the prison population by executing more criminals? Certainly we, as Jews, should be working for a better American penal system, both as individuals and as an organized Jewish community. Should we not give it priority attention, as we give to the security and survival of the State of Israel or attempts to bring Soviet Jews out of their "prison" in the Soviet Union? What would the prophets of Israel have demanded?

... and appointed you
A covenant-people, a light of nations—
Opening eyes deprived of light,
Rescuing prisoners from confinement,
From the dungeon those who sit in darkness.

Isa. 42:6–7

What do you think the prophet meant by this statement?

ABORTION

So far we have spoken about existing human life as we know it, the life of those already born and living on our planet. But there is a fierce controversy swirling around the questions of what life *is* and when life *begins.* Those are questions the prophets of Israel never had to face. For them it was a simple matter. Life was defined in terms of whether or not a person breathed. Life began the moment a human being emerged from the mother's womb. The knowledge of modern science has not only complicated those simple understandings; it has created a social controversy of major proportions. The dispute centers around whether or not a pregnant woman, who wishes not to have a baby she is carrying, may end that pregnancy by medical abortion without being accused of having committed a murder.

On January 22, 1973, the United States Supreme Court, in a historic and controversial decision, ruled that it was constitutional for a woman to have an abortion to prevent the birth of an unwanted child. They ruled that abortion could not be considered murder since "the Constitution does not define 'person' in so many words. The use of the word is such that it has application only postnatally. The unborn have never been recognized in the law as persons in the whole sense." That decision immediately touched off an enormous controversy in this country. There are religions, particularly Roman Catholicism, which do not agree with that definition. They believe that life begins at the very moment of conception. Thus, for them, abortion is nothing less than murder. As a result, millions of Americans have mounted intense campaigns to overturn the effects of that Supreme Court ruling and to prevent both the federal government and the states from giving financial aid to women who may wish or need an abortion.

When does life begin? That is the critical question underlying this dispute. If life begins at the moment of conception, than perhaps it would be fair to argue that to abort a fetus is to commit a murder. If however, life does not begin at that moment, there would be no reason why our legal system should prohibit abortion or treat it any differently from a host of other medical matters.

The matter of when life begins is not a new controversy. In ancient Greece, Aristotle held that life begins for males forty days after conception, and for females, ninety days after conception. Under Roman law, forty days was the determining point for both sexes. An abortion before that time was not considered murder. In the thirteenth century, Roman Catholic theologian St. Thomas Aquinas held that the beginning of life and soul occurred at the moment a baby first moved in the womb. It was not until 1869 that the Roman Catholic Church under Pope Pius IX proclaimed the doctrine of "immediate animation."

Neither is there total agreement on this issue in the world of science. Does life begin when sperm *reaches* egg, or when sperm *penetrates* egg? Is it when the chromosomes inside the egg and sperm pair, or when the fertilized egg begins to split for the first time? Or is it when the egg becomes attached to the wall of the womb, or even at some later stage? There is no way of deciding this old argument.

Judaism has its view, too. In Judaism, a fetus is not considered a full human being, and for this reason has no "juridical personality" of its own. In Judaism, the fetus in the womb is not a person *(lav nefesh hu) until it is born.* Up to the time of labor, the embryo and then the fetus is considered an organic part of the mother. Thus, in Judaism, life does not start at conception. Conception only gives *potential* for human life. According to Jewish law, a child is considered a "person" only when it is "come into the world." Thus, there is no capital liability for feticide. By this reckoning, abortion cannot be considered murder. The basis for this decision is scriptural. The biblical text states:

> When men fight, and one of them pushes a pregnant woman and a miscarriage results, but no other misfortune ensues, the one responsible shall be fined according as the woman's husband may exact from him, the payment to be based on reckoning. But if other misfortune ensues, the penalty shall be life for life. . . .
>
> Ex. 21:22–23

Talmudic commentators made the teaching of this biblical passage quite explicit. They said that only compensation in money is exacted of someone who causes a woman to miscarry. No prohibition is evident from this scriptural passage against destroying the unborn fetus. Clearly, and here the major rabbinic commentators on the Bible agree, the one who was responsible is not guilty of murder, *since the unborn fetus is not considered a person.* This concept is repeated in many different instances and in many different places in rabbinic writing. The classic source for this Jewish attitude toward the status of a fetus, and thus toward abortion, may be found in the Mishnah. Here it states: "A woman who is having difficulty in giving birth, it is permitted to cut up the child inside her womb and take it out limb by limb because her life takes precedent. (The principle of *rodeph* —the 'pursuer'—is applied in this instance. In problem pregnancies, the fetus is viewed as 'a pursuer,' which in seeking to be born is endangering the mother's life and must therefore be destroyed.) However, if the greater part of the child has come out, it must not be touched, because one life must not be taken to save another" (Mishnah Oholot 7:6).

Rashi, the preeminent commentator on the Bible and the Talmud, explains the talmudic passage as follows: "As long as the child did not come out into the world, it is not called a living being and it is therefore permissible to take its life in order to save the life of its mother. Once the head of the child has come out, the child may not be harmed because it is considered as fully born, and one life may not be taken to save another."

Despite this wealth of evidence from Judaism recognizing the legality of abortion, Orthodox Jewish authorities have taken and continue to take a negative view towards abortion. Indeed, Orthodox rabbis prohibit this act, except in such special instances as when a woman is impregnated through rape or incest, or when it is clear that continuation of the pregnancy to birth would constitute a clear danger to the health or life of the mother.

Were the beliefs of religion concerning abortion to be enacted into law, our right to follow our religious convictions as we understand them would be denied. This is a most serious matter since Jewish children are particularly subject to Tay-Sachs disease, a fatal genetic disease. No Tay-Sachs child has ever lived beyond the age of five years, and those afflicted die an agonizing death. Tay-Sachs disease cannot be detected until the third month of pregnancy and thus no therapeutic action can be taken until that time.

Reform Judaism has expressed itself quite clearly in favor of free choice in abortion. Basing its view on the totality of Jewish tradition, Reform Judaism agrees with the tradition and permits abortion when the life of the mother is at stake. However, it goes one step further and permits it even when the psychological well-being and mental health of the woman may be affected.

There are serious moral issues involved in the abortion question. If those who wish to make abortion illegal prevail, millions of women would bear unwanted children. Opponents of abortion have already succeeded in part, and the negative consequences are already being felt. In July 1977, the Supreme Court ruled that, while women do have the right to have abortions, the states *need not* pay Medicaid funds to poor women who seek abortions. Immediately twenty-six states discontinued Medicaid reimbursements. Several suspended the granting of payments. Only twelve states in our Union committed themselves to continuing such payments. As you might expect, the poor in our communities are most severely affected by these decisions. Yet, it is the poor who most frequently become pregnant without wanting to, and it is the poor who most desperately need financial help to end their pregnancies. Of the 1.2 million abortions performed in 1976, 300,000 of the women involved received Medicaid funds to pay for those abortions. Of that number, 85 percent were welfare mothers. Also of that number of 1.2 million, one-third of the females were teenagers and 15,000 were girls under fourteen years of age. Thus we can see that the ones who most need the financial help are the ones most denied.

Teenage pregnancy is fast becoming a problem of national disaster proportions. Children are becoming sexually active at an increasingly younger age. From 1940 to 1960, births in the 15–19 maternal age group doubled. Teenage pregnancy is now at a rate of one million a year. The fastest rise is in the youngest group, those 11–13 years of age.

The basic premise we cannot afford to overlook is that if the government will not pay for the abortion of a poor woman, whether or not she is a teenager, she cannot afford to go elsewhere. She is stuck. We are thus establishing one law for those who can afford to pay, while saying to the poor that they must abide by another. That, in our judgment, is discrimination of a most blatant and intolerable kind. What of *their* right to life?

The New Biology and its Implications

If we are not in agreement about when life begins, today there is even less certainty about when life ends. There is controversy concerning how to define it and what to do about keeping someone "alive" by use of the fantastic new medical technology available to us. Heart and lung machines can replace these organs, dialysis machines can assume the work of the kidneys, and respirators can continue the breathing that is normally done by lungs. Death is no longer the private matter it once was. In many instances the death of an individual is the failure of a machine or science.

As we have seen, Judaism teaches that life is good and that everything that can be done to maintain and preserve life ought to be done. But, Judaism also teaches that

> For everything there is a season . . .
> a time to be born, and a time to die . . . .
> Eccles. 3:1–2

Indeed, in Judaism the *quality* of life is as important as its mere being. Recently, the highest court in Massachusetts decided that life-prolonging treatments could be withheld from a patient diagnosed as having leukemia. The person was a sixty-seven year old mental retardee with a mental age of three. The majority of sixteen judges decided that such treatments were "extraordinary" and could be withheld. Had the patient in question been "normal" in other respects, the court might have demanded the continuation of the treatment.

Right to Die?

Not long ago a young girl from New Jersey named Karen Quinlan fell into a deep coma which continued for nearly two years. She was kept alive by a battery of special machines and scientific wizardry. But there was no chance for recovery. Finally, her parents asked first their physician and then the courts that she be taken off the machines and be given the "right to die with dignity." The doctors refused, insisting that it was their sworn obligation to prolong life as long as possible. But the parents demanded: "Does that mean that a person who has been reduced to a vegetable should be kept technically alive through 'heroic and extraordinary' medical methods even though her chances of recovering are nil? Shouldn't a person with a hopeless and mortal sickness be left to God to die in peace?"

Karen's case was taken to the courts and became a matter of great public controversy. Finally, the courts ruled: The artificial life support systems could be removed and nature left to take its course.

Judaism teaches that a dying person, no matter how ill and no matter how hopeless the situation, is still a living person in all respects. Nothing can be done to speed the dying process. However, Judaism does look sympathetically on *not* prolonging life by artificial means. There is a famous rabbinic story that deals with this issue. Rabbi Judah the Prince, author of the Mishnah and the greatest rabbi of his time, lay on his deathbed. Because his colleagues did not want him to die, they gathered under his window to pray for him. But, his servant-maid, seeing how helpless was his case and how much he was suffering, prayed that he be given the privilege of death. She asked the rabbis to stop their prayers so that Judah could die in peace. When they refused, she leaned out the window and threw down a huge earthen jar in order to disturb them and stop their prayers. Their prayers disrupted, Judah died. The rabbis praised her for this action, and from this case derived the law. One cannot artificially delay death (Ketuvot 104a).

Other rabbis, of a later period, expanded the principle. If one is chopping wood near the bed of a dying person, they said, and the patient is being kept alive by the noise which attracts his attention, then the woodchopper should be asked to stop. Similarly, one may not put salt (used as a stimulant) on the tongue of a dying person to revive him. Rabbi Nissim Gerondi even went so far as to say that there are times when one may ask God's mercy for a sick person to die. Quoting Ecclesiates, "a time to live and a time to die," another rabbi clearly stated that "one may pray for the death of another." Under Jewish law, which is the reflection and the embodiment of Jewish ethics, a physician may not force a terminal patient to live a few more days or a few more hours, only to endure suffering. Any machine, drug, or treatment should be begun and continued as long as doctors feel there is a chance of recovery. Once that no longer exists, doctors should feel free to remove or withhold such treatments.

It is a moral obligation to maintain life by all ordinary means, but there is no obligation to use extraordinary means. Ordinary means are actions which do not cause grave hardship to the patient and which offer a reasonable hope of success. Ordinary means of pursuing life include normal nursing care, feeding by mouth, giving fluids by mouth, and the relief of pain, insomnia, and mental anguish. Extraordinary means are those which offer no reasonable expectation of success or benefit. Extraordinary means are not likely to cure, they are unlikely to reverse the dying process, and they are repugnant to the family who come to see the patient as a machine kept alive merely by mechanical connections.

The most difficult question is the one that deals with who should decide in the matter of ending life support. Until now, it was the physician. The publicity surrounding cases like the Quinlan case has ended that practice. Doctors are afraid of being sued for malpractice by irate members of the family. Perhaps that is good. When the patient's mind is functioning, he or she should be given the right to make that decision. It is a right that belongs to the person and to no one else. Perhaps the decision can be made in advance through a living will. Many states now are considering "right to die" laws that will aid in that process. When the patient cannot be involved, it is the family who should be involved in making the decision.

We grant that this is a somewhat morbid topic, but it is better to face the realities of death than to pretend that death, and the pain that it brings, does not exist. The pain is mostly that of those who survive, and the real problems connected with death and dying do not affect the one whose life is ending as much as those who survive. Guilt is a frequent emotion felt by those who survive. "I didn't do enough." "I wasn't sensitive enough." "Why did it happen to him/her, not me?" Statements like these are all too frequently heard from family and friends who survive a death. There is a tragic, touching example of this sentiment in the Bible. King David's son Absalom had revolted against his father. In the course of that abortive effort, Absalom lost his life in a freak accident. Despite the son's revolt, David dearly loved Absalom. When news of his death was brought to the king, he broke down and cried bitterly:

> . . . My son Absalom! O my son, my son Absalom!
> If only I had died instead of you!
> O Absalom, my son, my son!
>
> 2 Sam. 19:1

Perhaps only someone who has lost a child can fully understand the anguish of that tearful lament.

Judaism does not encourage its practitioners to hide from the reality of death. On the contrary, every one of the rituals that Judaism expresses in connection with death is designed to force people to confront death's reality. In traditional Judaism, a person is buried as soon after death as possible. Only a plain wooden coffin is used. When it is lowered into the grave, it is broken apart to hasten the process of the decomposition of the body. The body, Judaism tells us, is only the container of the spirit. The body deteriorates, the spirit lives immortally. Survivors are encouraged to speak openly and at length about the dead. The entire process of sitting *shivah* (mourning for seven days immediately after death) is devoted to having those who survive talk out their feelings about the one who has died. Excessive grief is frowned upon. And after the mourning period is concluded, Judaism commands that we return fully to life and the tasks of living. We are commanded to remember the dead, but not to be possessed by death. Jewish thinking and practice faces death with openness and total honesty. We are commanded to grieve, to remember, but to return to the responsibilities of life as quickly as possible.

OUR RESPONSIBILITY TO OURSELVES

The burden of responsibility for our own health is increasingly coming to rest on ourselves. Are we ready to accept that responsibility? There is much evidence to suggest that the answer to that question is "no!" The National Cancer Institute estimates that close to 100,000 lives a year could be saved if Americans would stop smoking, drink less, and eat more roughage and less fat. The most difficult thing is to get people to do things for themselves and do them every day. Take smoking as an example.

TO SMOKE OR NOT TO SMOKE

Years of heavy research have now nailed down the fact that cigarettes *do* contribute to cancer and heart disease. The United States government issued very strong warnings to the people about the dangers of cigarette smoking but the manufacturers of cigarettes objected violently. They argued that people ought to have the right to choose for themselves. As a compromise, a warning label now appears on every package of cigarettes, and cigarette advertising has been banned from television. Despite all this, cigarette smoking, particularly among the young, increases each year at an alarming rate. Does this suggest that there may be a contempt for life among millions of people who seem to care more for their momentary pleasures than they do for their long-term health?

Should Judaism have anything to say about this situation? In a sense, traditional Judaism did and does. It prohibits any kind of smoking on the Shabbat. To be sure, the prohibition did not come into being because the rabbis knew that smoking caused an increase in cancer. It was prohibited because to light a match to a cigarette on the Shabbat was to "do work." Many synagogues and temples continue to prohibit smoking on their premises, and it is extremely offensive to smoke in front of or in the home of a traditional Jew on Shabbat and Yom Kippur. In light of what we now know about the harm that smoking does to the system, do you think this traditional Shabbat prohibition should be extended to all public places of the Jewish community? It is clear that Judaism prohibits and forbids any act which inflicts harm on one's body, even in the name of pleasure or freedom.

The body was too precious to be abused or treated with disrespect. After all, it was the container of the soul.

Should the organized Jewish community, particularly the organized Jewish religious community, support efforts to ban smoking? While there are some who believe so, most people believe a person should be free to decide for himself or herself. That is what the manufacturers of cigarettes say! Are they taking a principled position, or are they just using the ideal as a mask to cover their own desire to stay in business and make a profit? What would happen if cigarettes were made illegal? Did the law prevent people from drinking liquor during Prohibition? Does it prevent smoking pot and even more serious drug abuse today? Are there limits beyond which the law cannot go, especially when it comes to matters of personal behavior?

It is easy to laugh off the idea that Jewish tradition could make a difference to individual Jews when it comes to such a private decision as smoking or drugs. But it can. Take the similar problem of alcohol, another major health problem of our time. Judaism took a very characteristic position. It did not say that drinking in itself is wrong; it said that the *abuse* of drinking is wrong. Thus, wine is used as part of our religious ritual (the Kiddush on Shabbat, 4 cups at Passover, and so on). We drink a toast *(lechayim)* at joyous occasions. But the key was, and is, moderation. And believe it or not, that 3,000-year-old view of drinking has shaped the behavior of Jews in our time. Alcoholism is a massive health problem in the United States. Some 7 percent of all Americans are alcoholics; but less than 1 percent of Jews fall into that category. Why is that? It is because since biblical days each generation has handed down to the next generation a bundle of ideas—call it the Jewish way of life—and one of those has always been a powerful revulsion against excesses in alcohol (or anything else). By not trying to ban it outright, thus causing guilt feelings and the natural desire for the forbidden, Jews never made a big deal out of an occasional glass of wine or liquor by an adult, enjoyed in moderation like a *mensch* (human being). So Jewish values are not dead relics of ancient days; they underlie and shape our daily lives even today.

LIFE: THE SUPREME VALUE

But these Jewish life-affirming values are in conflict with many contrary values now moving in modern society. These include the demand for instant gratification here and now, the tendency to escape personal responsibility, the spread of "do your own thing" anarchy, and the popular denial of meaning and purpose in life. Life in the Jewish tradition is the paramount value, and the purpose of life is to create loving and caring human beings who are stewards of God's earth and nurturers of life for all God's creatures!

XIV

Epilogue

Y OU have met the prophets of Israel.

By now you should also better understand something of what they stood for, what they taught, the pain they experienced, the demands they made on their people, their courage, their anger, their failure.

Why have their messages survived? What can their words mean to us today? These are the inevitable questions of those who study the prophets.

The current period has been described as "me-ness" years; a period in which people turn inward, absorbed in themselves and in self-gratification. It is a time of the "Me Generation"; a period when individuals, disillusioned by corruption in government and private life, frustrated by the anonymous vastness of society, angered by relentless violence and insensitivity, have withdrawn to concentrate on themselves. The mood seems to be: "I want it all, and I want it now. To heck with anyone else. I'm looking out for number one." Even the ideal of being a good sport in the practice of athletics has almost disappeared. Sport in America today has become an amalgam of greed and brutality. Self-concern has become a national obsession. Basic structures of society suffer. Educational institutions deteriorate. The family seems to be collapsing as an institution; economic, ethnic, and racial groups polarize.

To anyone who has lived through these past twenty years, the difference between the 1980s and the 1960s is as dramatic as it is frightening. The decade of the sixties was a decade of causes. The issues of those years crowded into the lives of all whether they wanted them to or not. The justice and legality of the war in Vietnam was more than an academic question. The decision one made on those questions determined whether one went into the armed services or the anti-war movement, or maybe to Canada as a selective conscientious objector. The years following that fateful decade are not filled with the same demand for ethical decisions around large and obvious issues. The seventies were not years of causes. As a line in a recent film described it: "It's tough to even find a good cause nowadays."

The prophets of Israel lived through a time exactly like this one. They left us a fascinating description of the self-concern, even greedy selfishness, that characterized their age:

> Ah, you who are at ease in Zion
> And confident on the hill of Samaria,
> You notables of the leading nation
> On whom the House of Israel pin their hopes:
> Cross over to Calneh and see,
> Go from there to Great Hamath,
> And go down to Gath of the Philistines:
> Are [you] better than those kingdoms,
> Or is their territory larger than yours?
> Yet you ward off [the thought of] a day of woe
> And convene a session of lawlessness.
> They lie on ivory beds,
> Lolling on their couches,
> Feasting on lambs from the flock
> And on calves from the stalls.
> They hum snatches of song
> To the tune of the lute—
> They account themselves musicians like David.
> They drink [straight] from the wine bowls
> And anoint themselves with the choicest oils—
> But they are not concerned about the ruin of Joseph.
>   Amos 6:1–6

They are eager to do evil:
The magistrate makes demands,
And the judge [judges] for a fee;
The rich man makes his crooked plea,
And they grant it.

Mic. 7:3

This preoccupation with self was the reason above all others for which the prophets said Israel would be destroyed. When that destruction did come, it was this total self-concern that became the justifying cause:

The earth is withered, sear;
The world languishes, it is sear;
The most exalted people on earth languish.
For the earth was defiled
Under its inhabitants;
Because they transgressed teachings,
Violated laws,
Broke the ancient covenant.

Isa. 24:4–5

Some feel that contemporary civilization is on the verge of a similar collapse. Many people, especially those who live in our large urban centers, fear that the quality of life has deteriorated to such a point that it may be irretrievable. One writer described his feelings:

The plague is upon us in full force. The blatant attacks on our citizens are the open sores, the overt symptoms. The plague itself runs deep; it touches the very soul of man, which has turned away from itself.

We have shaped a mechanical Moloch in whom we put our faith and hope—even our definition. We have created a civilization that inundates man with worthless paraphernalia, producing ten of what nobody really needs one of, and withholding what people cannot do without. What ails us within ourselves, we ascribe to forces without—and trust that our ever proliferating machinery will make well.

Thus the plague has come—spawned in the decay of man's soul. Violence is upon us; from the merciless apathy of governments toward human suffering to the vengeful strike of the psychopathic murderer; from the ruthless aggrandizement of the corporate giants to the stealthy mugger, from organized state terror to organized crime, from the criminal acts of rapists, kidnappers, arsonists, air pirates and drug pushers to the lethal acts of vehicular crime on the highways; from the neglect and abuse of our children . . . to the callous revilement of our handicapped and wholesale junking, like scrap, of our elderly.

We shrink from seeing the real picture: the impotence of our religions, the moribundity of our social forms, the bankruptcy of our educational institutions, the absurdity of our economic systems, the hypocrisy of our "morals," . . . the absence of our feelings. We refuse to look inward and view the rot, preferring instead to gaze at our "tangible, real" world—the incredible profusion of technological refuse for which we have bartered away life . . . .

I hear ever more loudly the rumbling of the New Barbarians we have bred in our dispirited, soulless civilization.

They draw closer.

One day they will cross the river and topple Rome.
    Chayym Zeldis, "Anti-Perspirants Won't Help,"
        The New York Times, May 1, 1977

Are those who evaluate society in such doomsday terms correct? Muster as many facts on both sides of the issue as you can, and debate the issue for yourselves.

And if civilization is falling apart at the seams, what should our response be? Measure our ideal response against our actual behavior. Does our actual life-style reflect our true beliefs about the quality of life?

And if we reject the thesis that the quality of life is deteriorating to a point of no return, how do we express that rejection? What values do we exhibit that affirm the value of life?

Some, mostly young people, picket sites where nuclear plants are being built. Are they right in doing so? If nuclear energy is the way to free us from dependence on fossil fuels —some of which, like oil, may be totally expended before your life span is over—shouldn't its use and the building of facilities to generate nuclear energy be encouraged rather than opposed? But after the Three Mile Island near-disaster, can we believe that nuclear energy is safe?

What do we do to conserve energy? Are we involved in programs or projects that preserve our fragile ecology? Do we recycle waste material? What do we do to express the psalmist's prophetic conviction that "the earth is the Lord's and the fulness thereof, the world and those who dwell therein" (Ps. 24:1)? In short, how does our life-style reflect our sense of values?

A few who accept dire predictions of things to come in the imminent future have taken to the hills, waiting for the "day of judgment." The majority of the doomsayers, however, stay where they are, resigned to what they consider the unalterable slide of society into oblivion. Some, in frustrated anger, destroy what and where they are. They seem to reason that since life isn't worth much, since they are faceless nobodies, who cares about a society which has reduced them to such a condition? The raw quality of their actions provokes fear and hostile condemnation. But others, possessed of similar convictions and with greater means, behave in equally selfish but more socially acceptable ways. They don't tear down, burn, riot, or loot. They simply exploit. Take! Live it up! Travel! Acquire! Waste! Let the next generation worry about itself. I want it all for myself and I want it now. Paradoxically, theirs has become acceptable behavior.

How would the prophets of Israel have responded to this contemporary condition?

Everything we know about them suggests that they would find us morally wanting. They would denounce the establishments that allowed any segment of the population to be so repressed that it lost it's sense of self-worth. They would rail against the hedonistic pursuit of self-pleasure. Anything that robbed human beings of their dignity was, for them, an insult against the Divine. One can almost hear them on any main street, shouting out their truths about *our* generation:

> I bade you seek justice, and behold you have fashioned a cesspool you call civilization.
> Woe to those who lie on beds of ivory
> and straighten their heads with liquor and drugs.
> You have ground the face of the poor in the dust
> and the reek of violence is everywhere in the land.
>
> I commanded you to pursue peace and behold
> You have killed one another in the name of defense.
> You have put your trust in neutron bombs
> and call this a generation of peace.
> My eyes are affronted by the work of your hands.
> My lakes and my rivers which sparkled with joy
> are become desolate and foul
> You have blasphemed the glories of my creation
> invaded the cool calm of my forests
> and laid them bare for private gain.
> You have tarnished my air, polluted my water.
>
> You call My name constantly
> But none takes Me to their heart.
> I hate I despise your feasts
> I take no delight in your solemn assemblies
> Return unto the Lord
> For you have stumbled in your inequity.

Unfortunately, the denunciation would probably fall on deaf ears. Denunciation is no longer an effective technique. Even some believers in God seem no longer prepared to accept any given law code as Divinely revealed. Many would insist on the right and the duty to interpret past traditions. Those who call out in God's name "You shall" or "You shall not" can expect to be challenged immediately by the questions: "Why? Who says?"

Other factors also inhibit our acceptance of prophetic utterances. In the first place, ethical attitudes and beliefs are no longer shaped solely or primarily by religious teachings. Other motivations enter in, including personal experiences and emotional needs, such as fear of disapproval or rejection and the desire to be loved or accepted. We call these "psychological forces." Their effect on the way we shape our ethical decisions is as potent, if not more so, as the power of religious teaching. That is why it is so hard to *teach* values. They are frequently in conflict with more powerful subjective personal emotions.

Moreover, modern life sets before us a bewildering assortment of values, which are frequently in conflict with one another. We may want to choose the proper course of action, but we may not know what that is. Recently, a man allowed his friend of 39 years to commit suicide in his home. The man was 75 years old, a physician suffering from an incurable case of Parkinson's disease. "He came to me because I was his friend and because I would guard his right to do this . . . He could take the pills himself. No problem there. But to give him the comfort and the peacefulness of being with a friend in his last days and to make sure that he was not thwarted, this was very important."

Since Pennsylvania law did not consider suicide a crime, he invited the doctor to come to his home. After five pleasant and peaceful days together, during which they worked out many legal details, the doctor retired one night after dinner, bade farewell to his friend, and swallowed a lethal dose of Seconal. He died in his sleep (*The New York Times,* December 10, 1977).

This story was reported by the friend to the tenth annual meeting of the Euthanasia Educational Council, an organization that endorses what is commonly called "mercy killing."

Was this an ethical act on the part of the doctor? His friend?

Judaism would say no. But what would you say? How would you decide? What criteria would you apply?

ACTIONS AND CONSEQUENCES

The prophets of Israel would have asked: What are the consequences? They saw humanity's world as governed by the law of consequence. As we have tried to show, the prophets believed that there was a meaning and a purpose to events.

> History is not merely a chronicle of occurrences, a chain of unrelated incidents. On the contrary, they believed that history has a direction, a goal and, therefore, there is a meaning behind the bewildering complexity of human events. The prophets saw man's world as governed by the laws of consequence which, in perhaps oversimplified form, declares that right doing leads to well-being and wrong doing to disaster.... The biblical tradition maintains that we live in a universe in which righteousness is the basic law of human experience. This law cannot be violated by society with impunity, any more than a builder can permanently disregard the laws of gravitation without suffering the penalty. There often is a delay from the time the sin is committed until the consequence appears, but sooner or later it must happen.
> Robert Gordis, "A Basis for Morals: Ethics in a Technological Age," *Judaism*, p. 41

While Dr. Gordis is describing the prophetic attitude toward social trends, the theory applies also to what individuals do and do not do. In light of this, can one condone the euthanasia incident described above?

Many of the ethical dilemmas raised by the prophets which we have put before you in this book are abstractions, removed from our personal lives. While it is true that our attitude toward euthanasia, capital punishment, abortion, or mechanical life support systems depends on our attitude toward the meaning and essence of life, and while it is hoped that these attitudes might be shaped by what religion teaches us, few of us ever have to test our attitudes by applying them directly to life or death situations. How often are

any of us called upon to decide whether someone should live
or die? How many of us will ever have to decide whether or
not to "pull the plug" on a living being? But some of us will
have to make some of these decisions at some point in our
lives. We may be called to jury duty in a case involving
capital punishment. We or our mates may need or want an
abortion. Some of us may become doctors and have to make
a Karen Quinlan-like decision. All of us are certainly faced
with daily decisions about truth-telling or stealing when we
know we will not be caught. How shall we decide what to
do? Does the prophetic principle of the law of consequences
apply? What effect do others have on our decision-making
process? There was a time when what society thought of our
actions made a very great difference. When social groupings
were small, when what we did and did not do was known
to those with whom we lived and who knew us, society
shaped our ethical responses. It was called "peer pressure."
Today anonymity and the erosion of ethical standards gives
peer pressure an opposite, perhaps negative thrust. How
hard it is to say no to the offer of a drag on a joint when
everyone else in the gang is sitting around, getting high.
How hard it is to say no to sexual advances when "everybody
does it nowadays." How hard it is for adults to avoid padding
their expense statements when everybody is doing it!

Everyone! Everybody else! *Terrifying words.* Peer
pressure. Few can resist it. Only prophets. They were lonely
people. But no one is expected to be a prophet nowadays,
and loneliness is to be avoided like the plague!

In a generation where self-gratification and self-indul-
gence are the expected and accepted goals, ethical role
models are woefully absent. The model of the good Samaritan, who comes to the aid of a fellow human being, is often
considered a fool. That person seems always to end up shot,
beaten, or so entangled in bureaucratic red tape or negative
publicity that the involvement turns out to be either tragic
or ludicrous. Under such circumstances, most people reason
that it is better to stay out: "Look out for number 1." "This

business about being my brother's keeper is for the birds."

Society can create either a positive or negative climate for ethical response. It can encourage or discourage individual courage, dissent, critical thought. In a community where social concern has eroded, it is harder to act ethically. It is certainly more difficult to speak and act prophetically.

Perhaps such a condition obtains in the American Jewish community. A kind of collective "me-ness" seems to permeate the psyche of Jews. We, too, seem totally self-concerned. There is little room on the agenda of our community organizations for issues other than Israel, Soviet Jewry, and defending against perceived eruptions of anti-Semitism. What about the universal, human, prophetic agenda?

Running against the stream brings pain and the threat of social ostracism. Few today wish to expose themselves to that. We are not so naive as to think that people are going to mold their lives on the patterns of an Amos, Isaiah, or Jeremiah. That is too difficult. The prophets failed in their day, not because what they preached was wrong, but because what they demanded was too difficult. Their messages survive precisely because they were right and, above all, acutely relevant to every succeeding age.

Thus, *moral freedom* is the basis of human responsibility for one's actions. Without moral freedom, society cannot exist. In other words, reason as an intellectual concept is the equivalent of freedom in the moral sphere and of responsibility in the social realm. No ethical system can dispense with this assumption of our moral freedom. People can and must choose. What Judaism can bring home to us is the conviction that people faced with choice can be assured that Divinity summons us to moral conduct.

God's ultimate character, insofar as humans may speak of such exalted matters, is not neutral. God is not to be approached through a realm that ultimately lies beyond morality. God's holiness is intimately linked with God's ethical

command. There is a direct movement from "You shall be
holy for I the Lord, your God, am holy" to "You shall not
hate your brother in your heart, but you shall love your
neighbor as yourself." . . . We are summoned and sent and
judged and held accountable—and in just such moral sua-
sion we also see the signs of God's close caring.

Eugene Borowitz, "America's Moral Crisis," *Worldview,*
Nov. 1974, p. 54

What all this means is that we can choose a positive moral
identity with some assurance that it reflects the Divine.
What then shall we choose? We can choose to care about
what goes on about us. No one can be fully alive who is not
passionately concerned with what goes on around one or
who fails to see what happens to other people. Caring is the
first step toward involvement. It is the first antidote to isola-
tion and exclusivity.

We can accept a measure of personal responsibility for
what goes on around us, in our families, our classes, our
clubs, our town, and eventually our world. "The buck stops
here" is a good motif for everybody, not just presidents. We
may not be able to affect a national revolution in morality
but we can, by our actions and interests, begin to add a bit
to changing the atmosphere of our society.

We can identify with the Jewish people. Judaism and
its carrier, the Jewish community in its totality is and always has been a force for human values on this planet. By
identifying ourselves with that community, we become
part of a continuum of eternal value. Only by identifying
with this Jewish people can we achieve a measure of im-
mortality.

We can refuse to accept denigration and contempt for
life. The silent spectator who tolerates and does not protest
is as dangerous as the bigot and the thief. Silence makes one
an accomplice to brutality and barbarism. It adds to the
violation of the quality of life. By refusing to capitulate, by
refusing to follow the multitude to do evil, we purify the

moral atmosphere. That may be much more important than the achievement of an empty popularity.

Finally, we can maintain our faith in God and God's humanity, and in its limitless possibilities. The world may be sick, but we are not sliding down the slippery slope to oblivion. If there is trouble in our land and world, it has been said it is better to light a candle than to curse the darkness. The biggest lie that is told is that we cannot change human nature. Human nature is certainly one of the things we *can* change. The prophets were often filled with despair, but they did not resign from the human race or abandon their belief that humanity could grow and mature. Giving up on people and on life is the ultimate retreat. It is unworthy. Worse, it is suicidal. It is anti-Jewish.

Each of us has an opportunity to leave a footprint in the moral clay of life. It is hoped that each of us will walk in such a way as to cause others to follow in our path. Micah said it best: "He has told you, O man, what is good, And what the Lord requires of you. Only to do justice and to love goodness and to walk modestly with your God" (Mic. 6:8). The finest things that can ever be said of any of us are:

> "That's a person I can trust."
> "I can believe in him/her."
> "I can put my faith in him/her."
> "That's a good person!"

Put in prophetic language, it would sound like this:

> This is My servant, whom I uphold,
> My chosen one, in whom I delight.
> I have put My spirit upon him,
> He shall teach the true way to the nations.
> He shall not cry out or shout aloud,
> Or make his voice heard in the streets.
> He shall not break even a bruised reed,
> Or snuff out even a dim wick.
> He shall bring forth the true way.

He shall not grow dim or be bruised
Till he has established the true way on earth;
And the coastlands shall await his teaching.
Thus said God the Lord,
Who created the heavens and stretched them out,
Who spread out the earth and what it brings forth,
Who gave breath to the people upon it
And life to those who walk thereon.

                                    Isa. 42:1–5

Commission on Jewish Education
of the
Union of American Hebrew Congregations
and
Central Conference of American Rabbis

MARTIN S. ROZENBERG, CHAIRMAN

SOLOMON B. FREEHOF, HONORARY CHAIRMAN

DOROTHY G. AXELROTH
MORTON A. BAUMAN
STEPHAN F. BARACK
HERBERT M. BAUMGARD
ALAN D. BENNETT
MURRAY BLACKMAN
HOWARD BOGOT
GENA BRAGIN
STEPHEN BRAGIN
ERIC FELDHEIM
HARVEY J. FIELDS
LEON GILDESGAME

ROLAND B. GITTELSOHN
JUDITH HERTZ
LAWRENCE HOFFMAN
JACK HOROWITZ
JILL ISCOL
SAMUEL K. JOSEPH
SAMUEL E. KARFF
LYDIA KUKOFF
JANET W. LERNER
AUDREY FRIEDMAN MARCUS
KENNETH MIDLO
ROBERT ORKAND

STEVEN M. REUBEN
KENNETH ROSEMAN
BERNICE RUDNICK
LENORE SANDEL
CAROLYN SCHOENBERG
FREDERICK C. SCHWARTZ
L. WILLIAM SPEAR
MARTIN STRELZER
M. ROBERT SYME
MARTIN S. WEINER
FLORA WINTON
JOEL I. WITTSTEIN
RAYMOND A. ZWERIN

Ex Officio

WILLIAM CUTTER
DONALD S. DAY
A. STANLEY DREYFUS
LEON FRAM
JOSEPH B. GLASER
JEROME R. MALINO

RICHARD MORIN
EARL MORSE
ALEXANDER M. SCHINDLER
PAUL M. STEINBERG
ELLIOT L. STEVENS
BERNARD M. ZLOTOWITZ

UNION EDUCATION SERIES
Edited by
DANIEL B. SYME, *National Director of Education*

Director of Publications
Stuart L. Benick